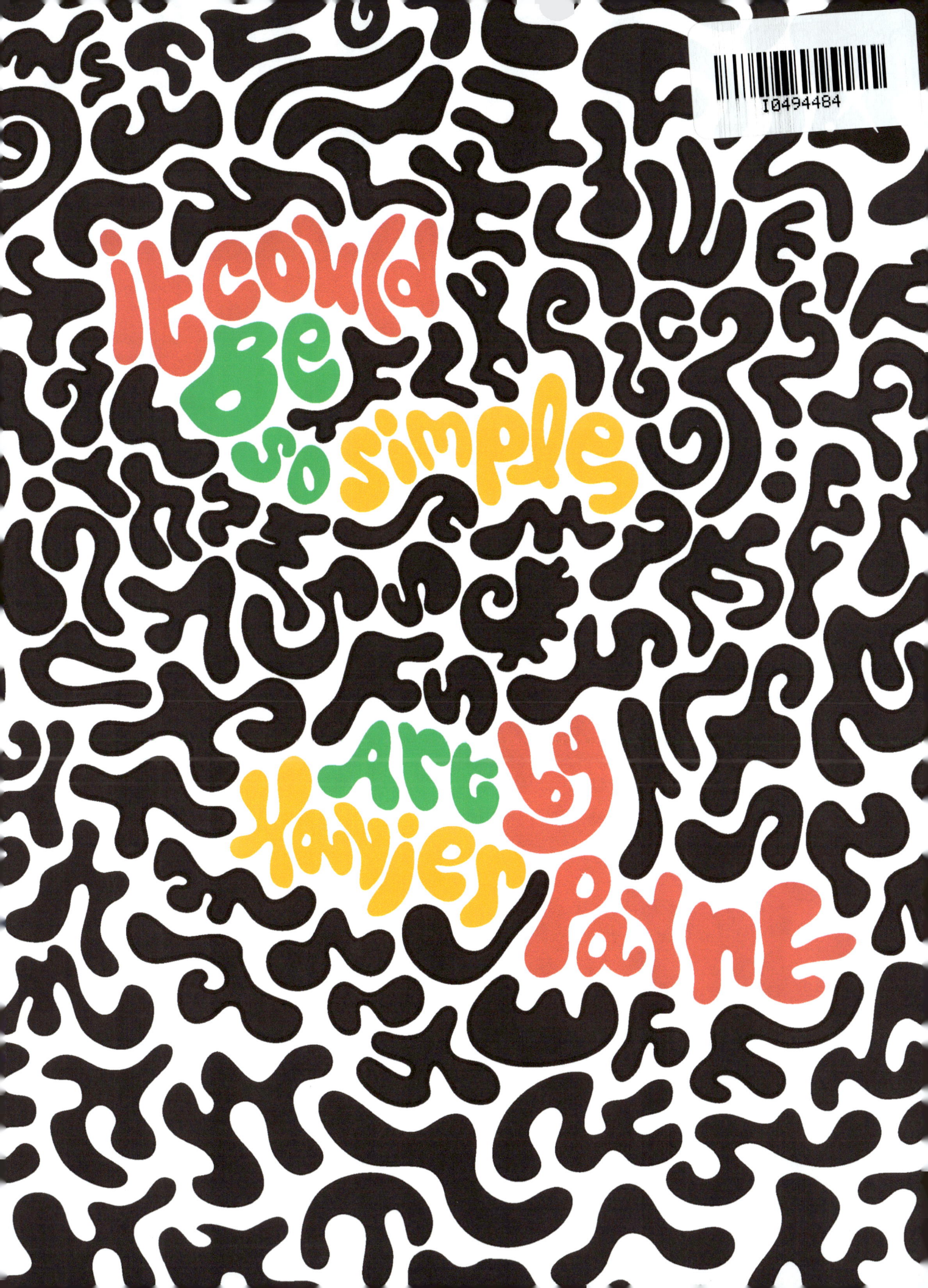

it could Be so simple

Art by Xavier Payne

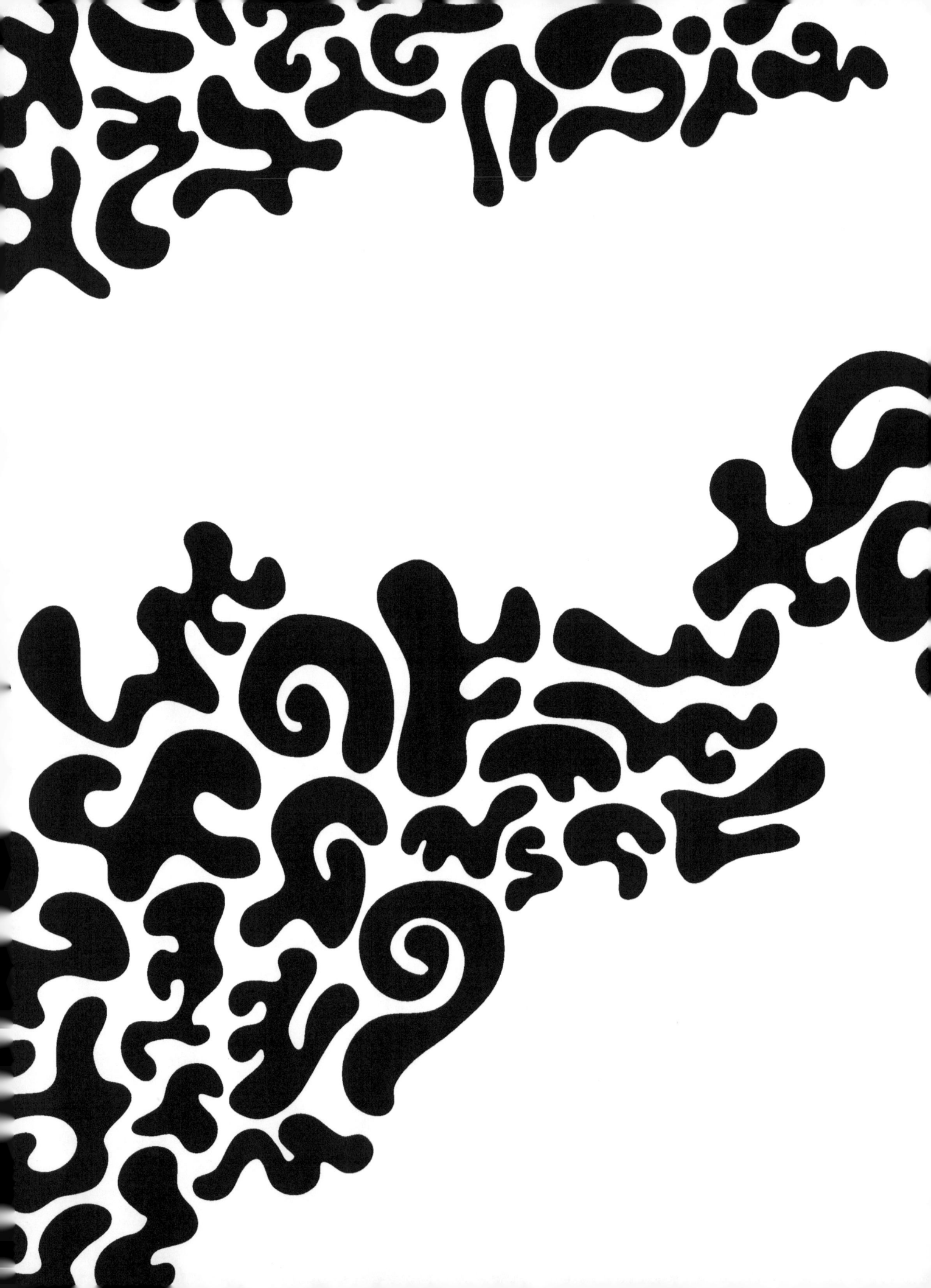

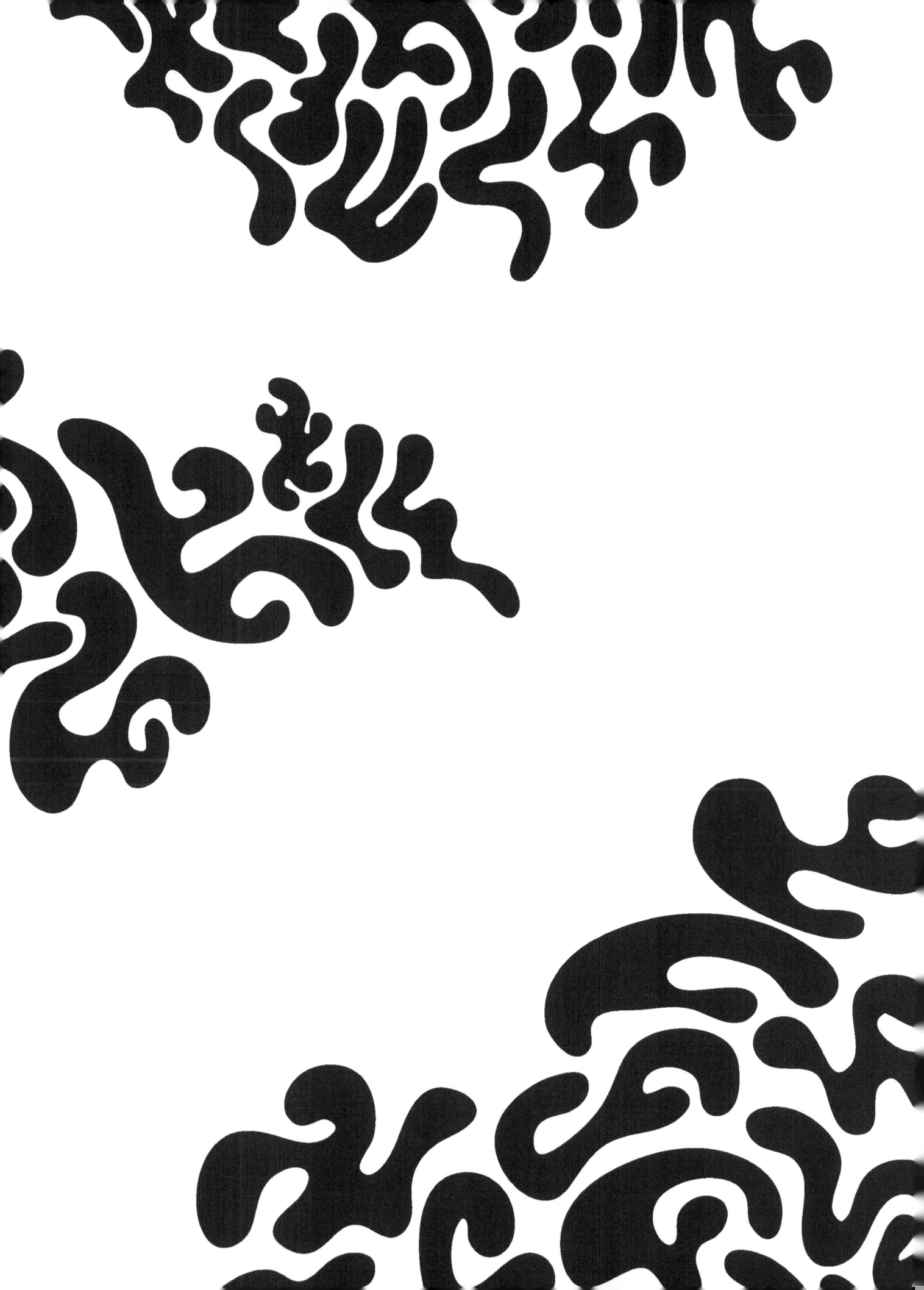

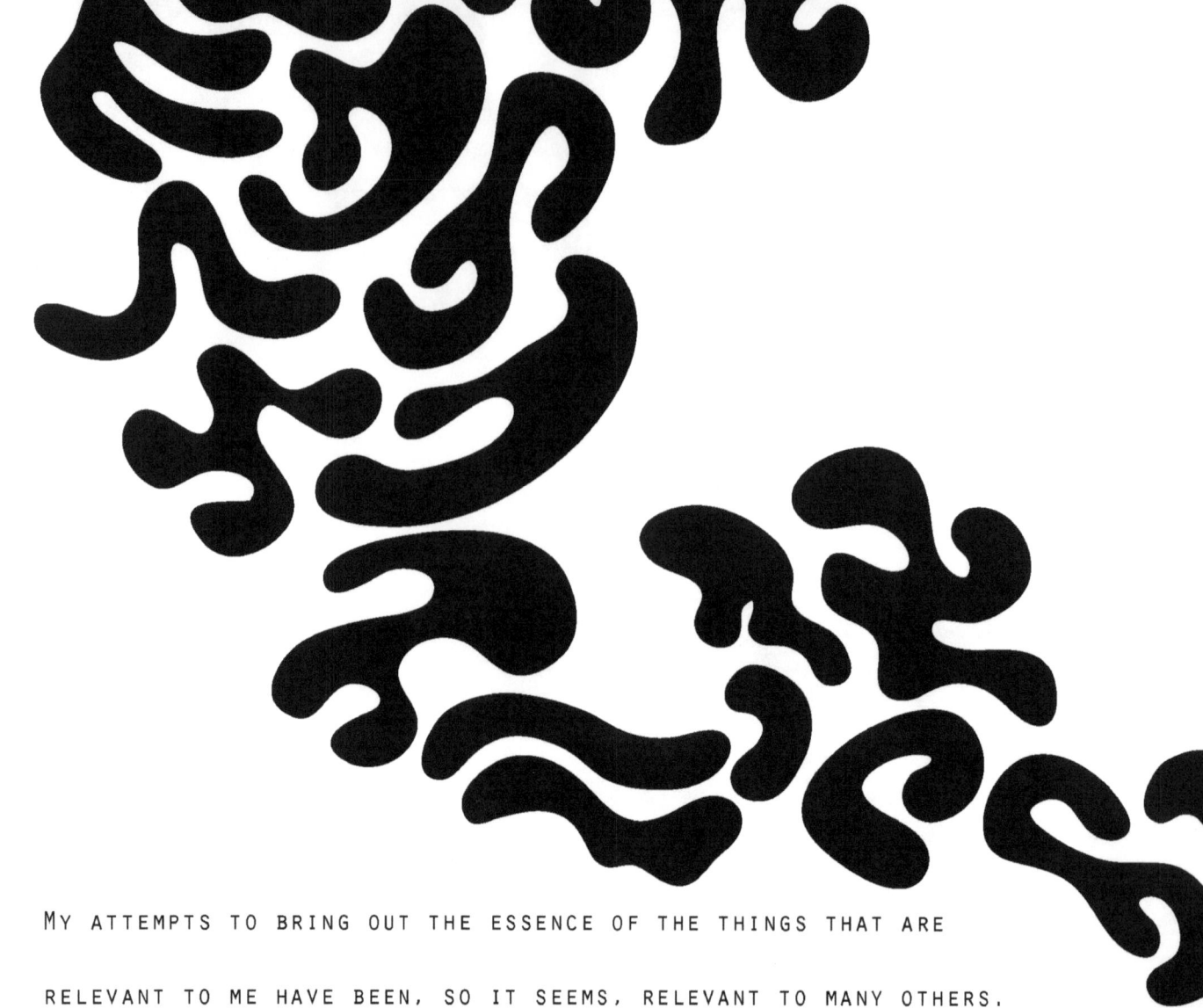

My attempts to bring out the essence of the things that are relevant to me have been, so it seems, relevant to many others. Since I am not SO different from you, I imagine that you have fears, doubts, anxieties, long days, and things of the like. These layers tend to to complicate life of course. But things could be so much simpler.

I try to show that, visually.

My name is Xavier Payne, and I illustrate, draw, design, paint, and create visually based forms of art.

THIS BOOK IS A COLLECTION OF ILLUSTRATIONS, SKETCHES, AND DRAWINGS FROM 2013-2014.

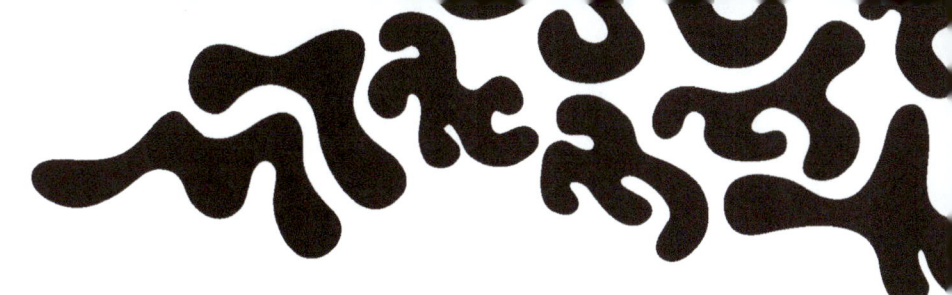

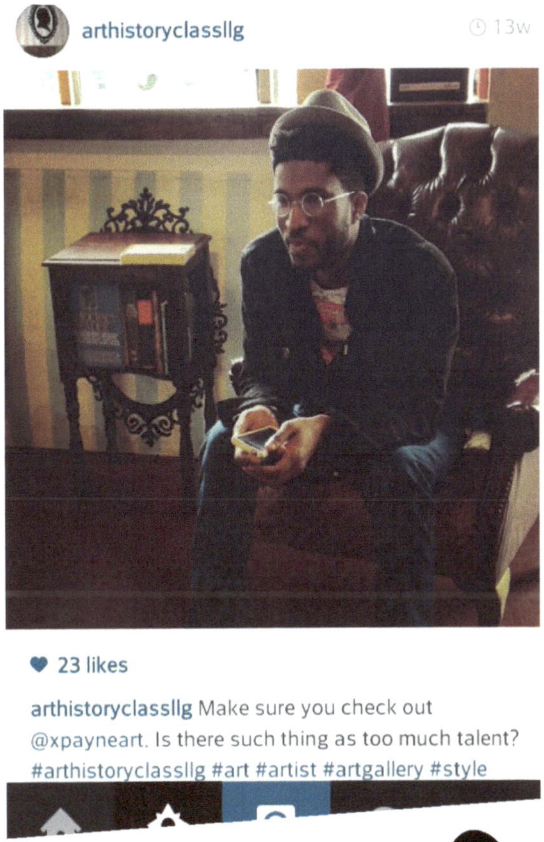

arthistoryclassllg   13w

♥ 23 likes

arthistoryclassllg Make sure you check out @xpayneart. Is there such thing as too much talent? #arthistoryclassllg #art #artist #artgallery #style

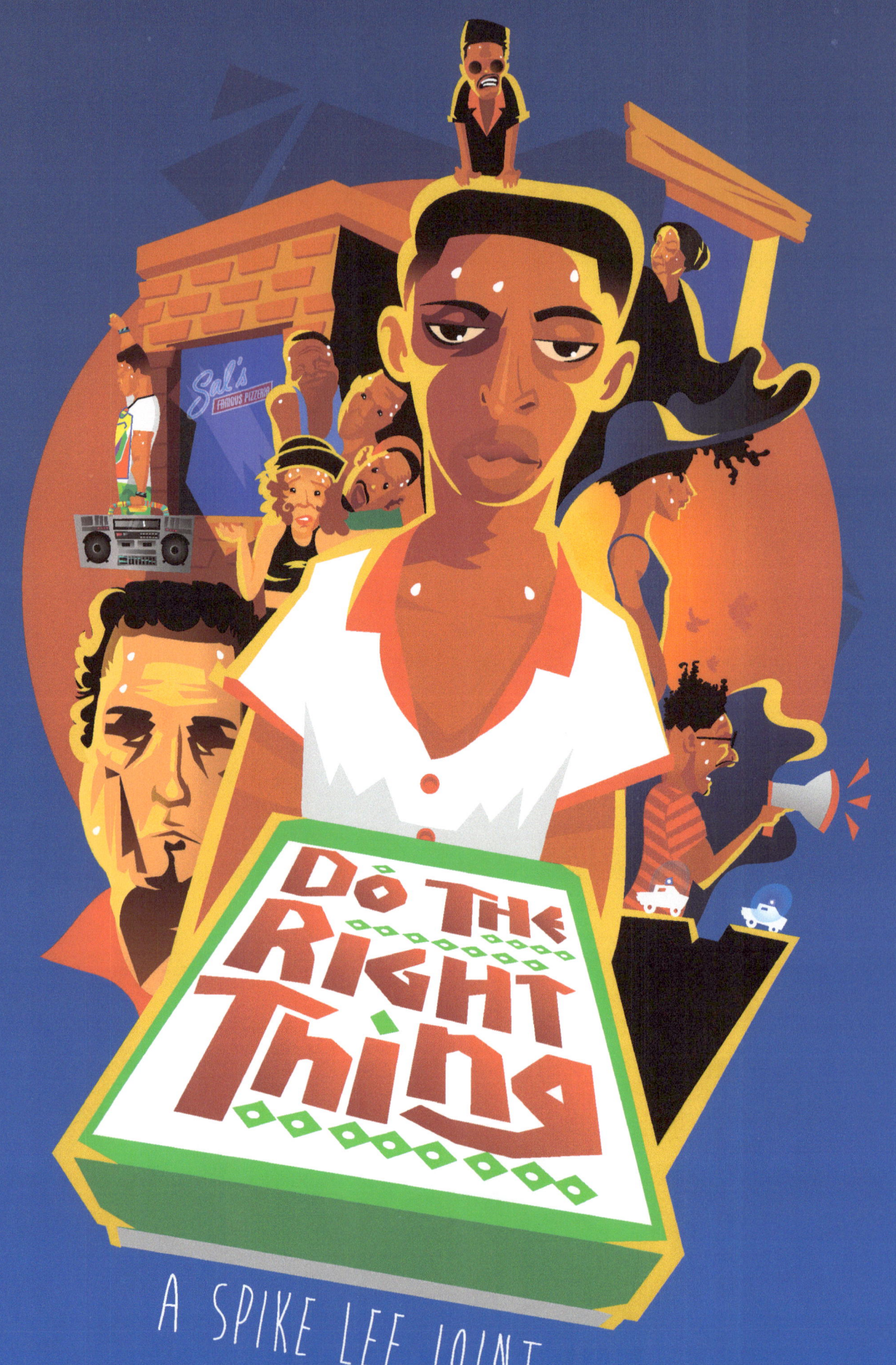

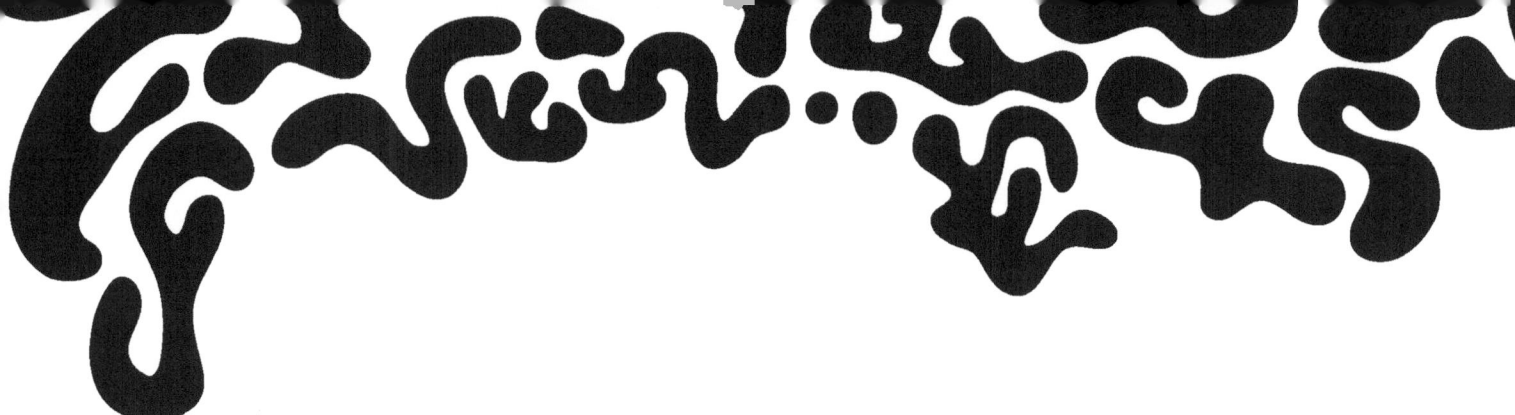

THE 90S/POP ART*

EVERY GENERATION LOOKS BACK ON ITS HEYDAY. I SIMPLY WANTED TO STAY AS
CLOSE TO MY CHILDHOOD AMBITIONS AS POSSIBLE, BECAUSE MY POTENTIAL WAS
BOUNDLESS AND IGNORANCE WAS AN OPPORTUNITY FOR WISDOM.

X

* ONE PIECE IN THIS BOOK DOES

FEATURE A 1970's ICON. I

INCLUDED IT IN THIS

GROUP OF WORK.

BLACK
FRAKENSTEIN!!!

Look inside th
PAUL MCARTNEY
MAN C

Kehinde

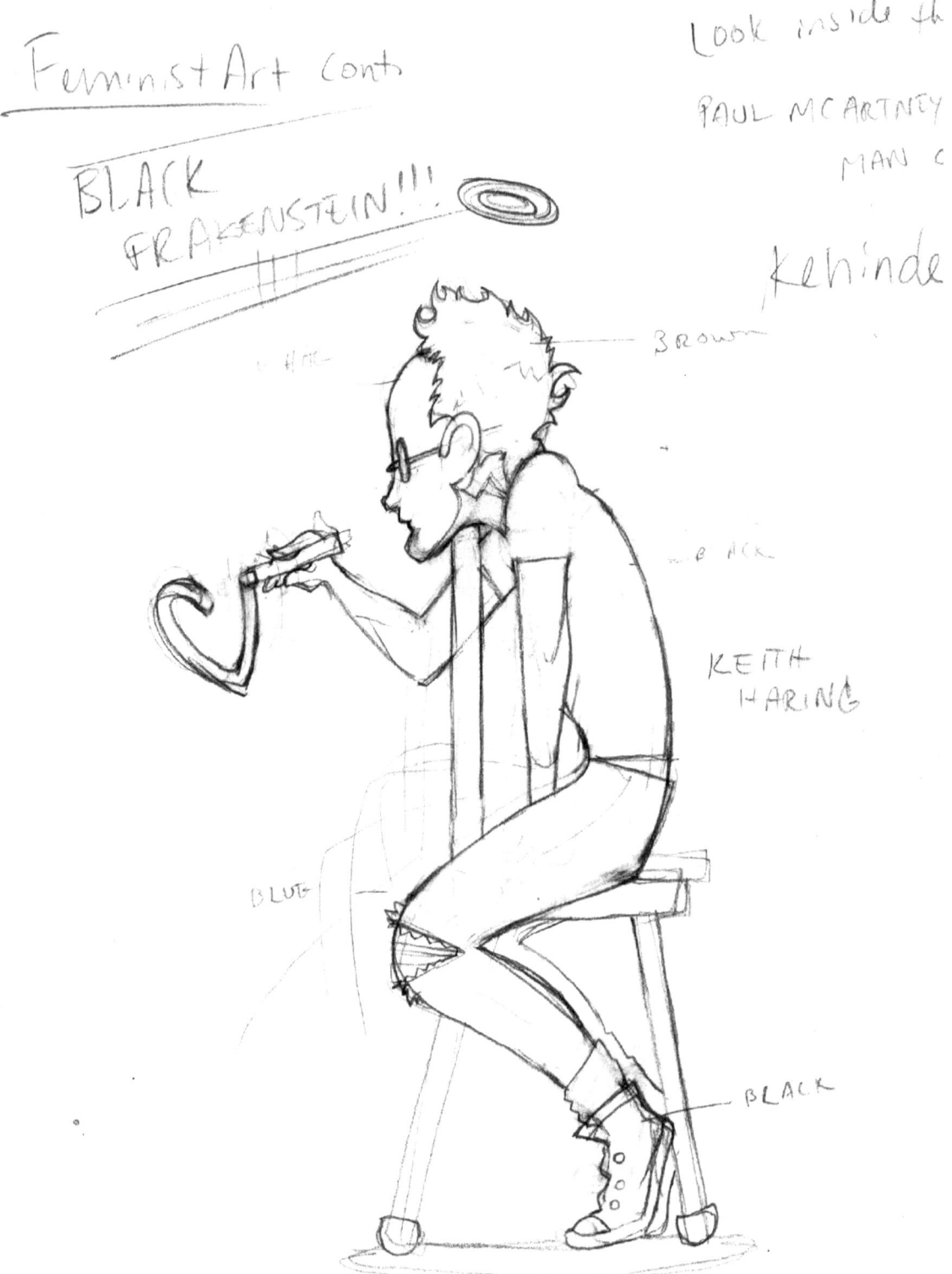

BROWN

HAIR

BLACK

KEITH
HARING

BLUE

BLACK

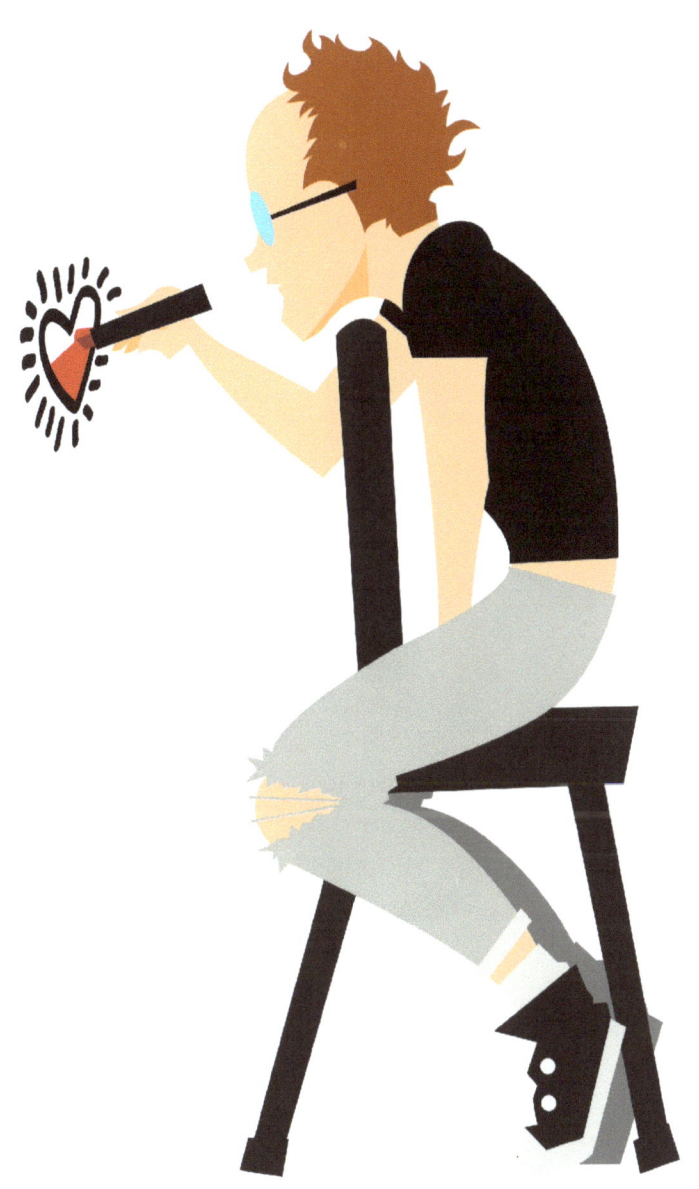

KEITH KARING

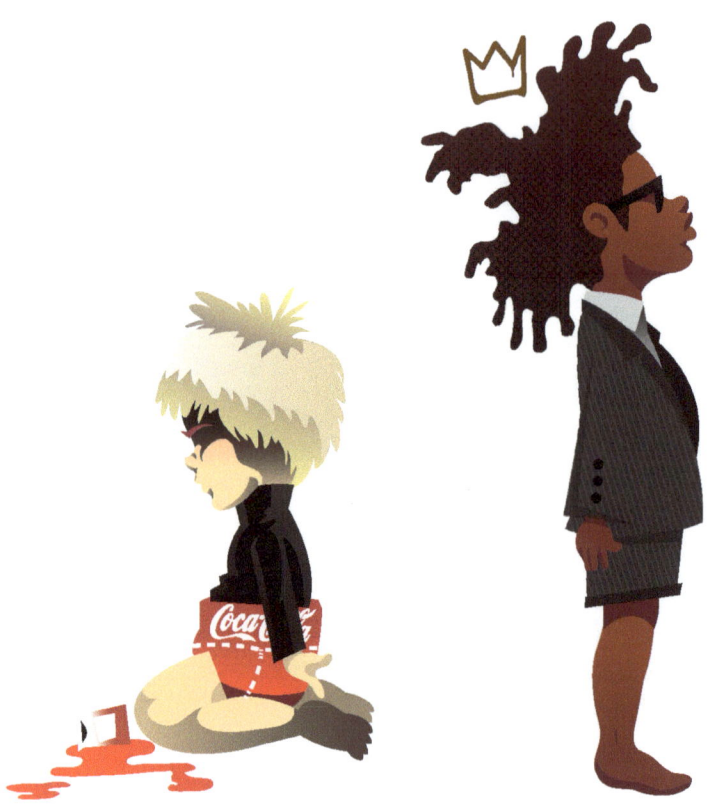
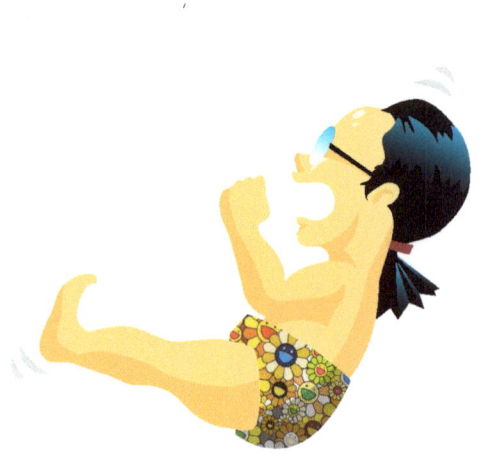

BABY WARHOL, KID JMB, BABY TAKASHI MURAKAMI

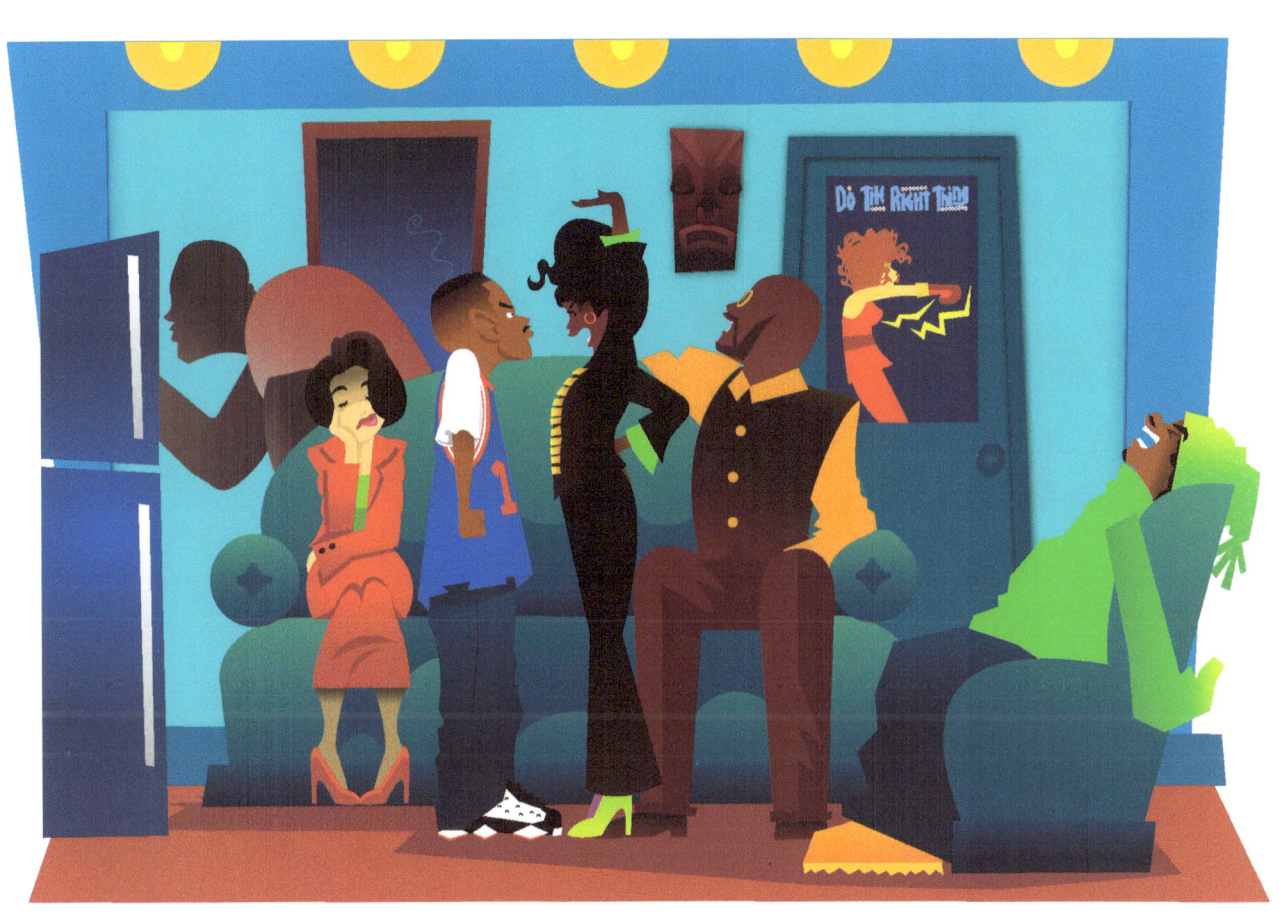

SHORTY BY NATURE

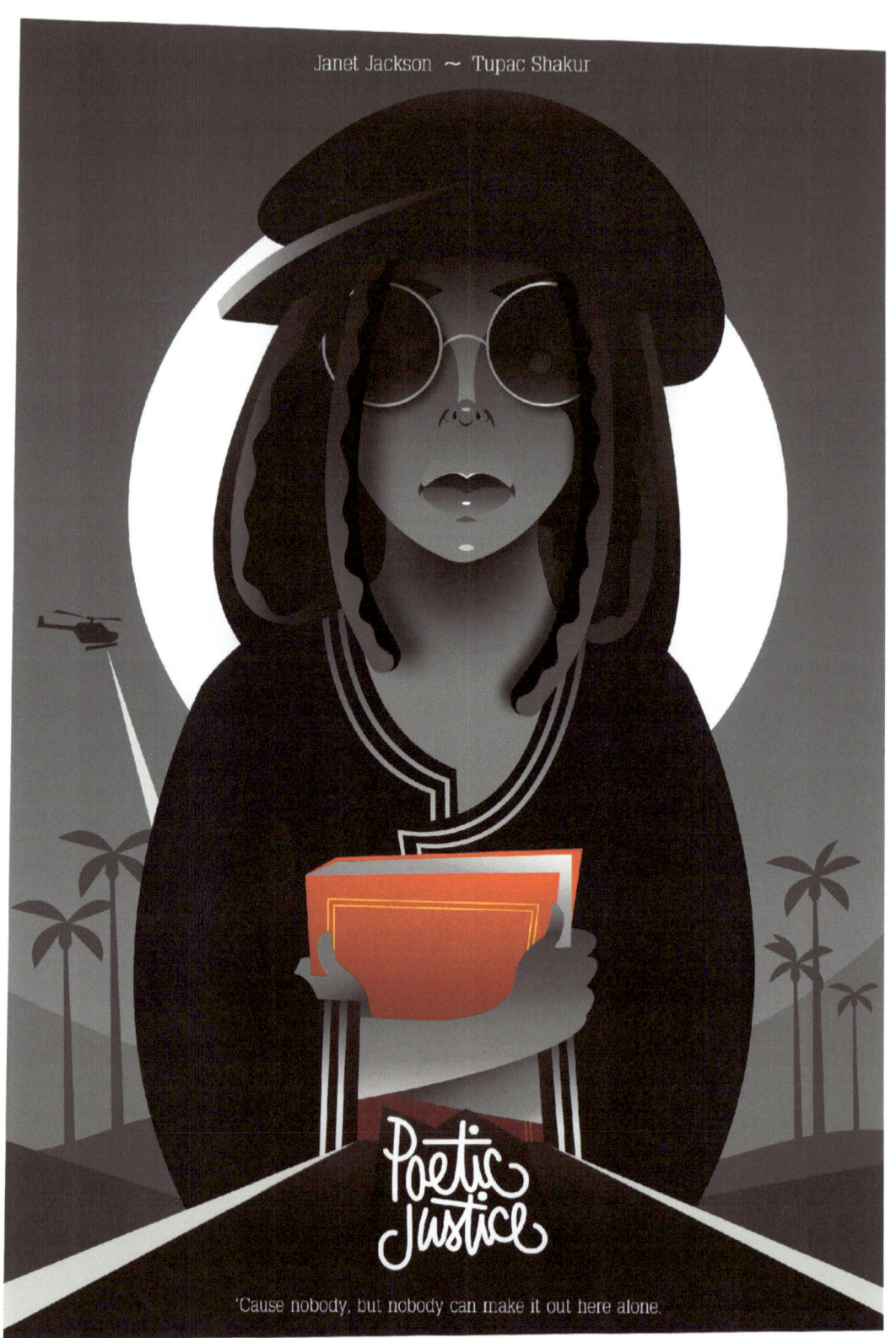

POETIC JUSTICE

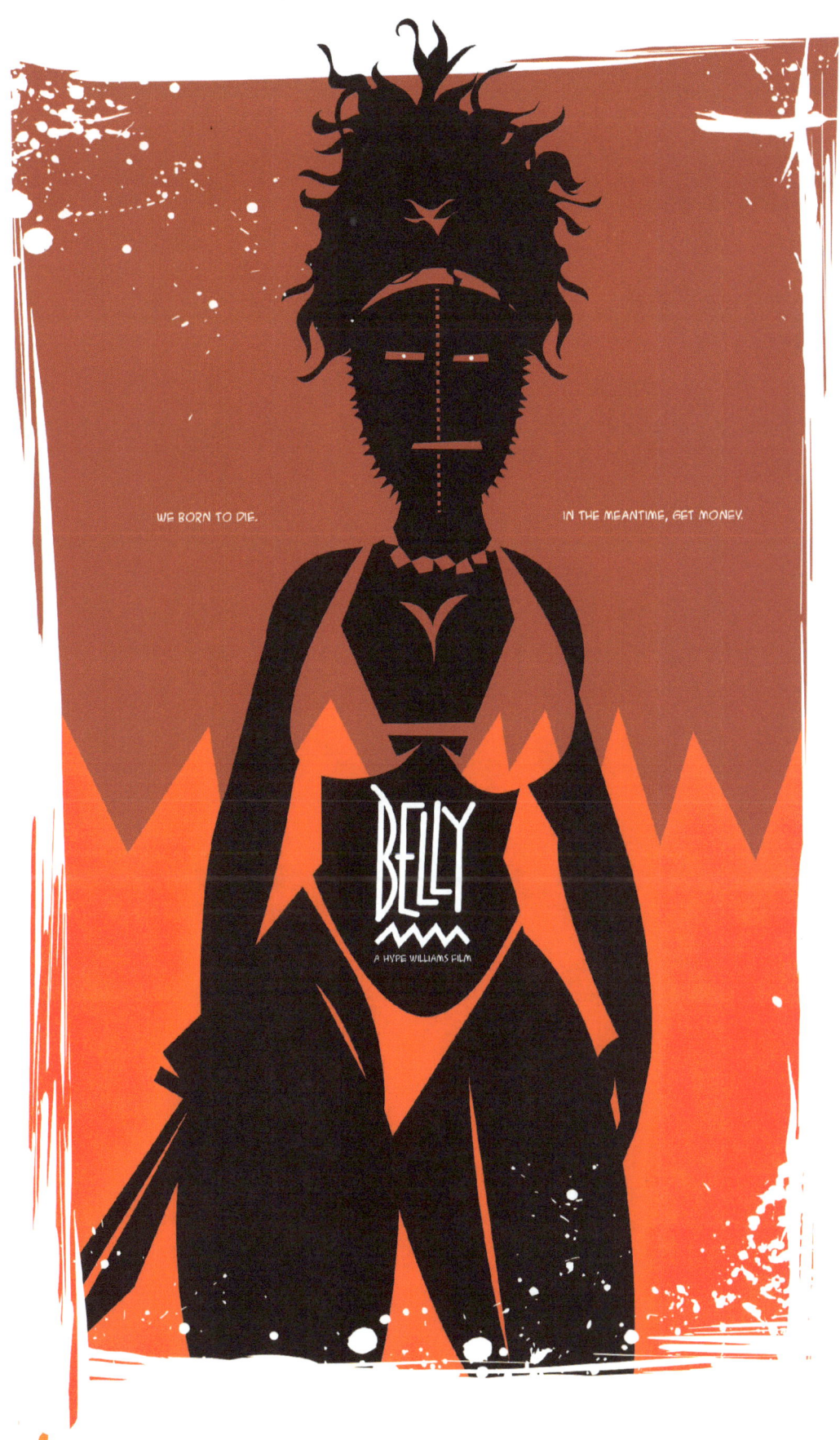

BELLY

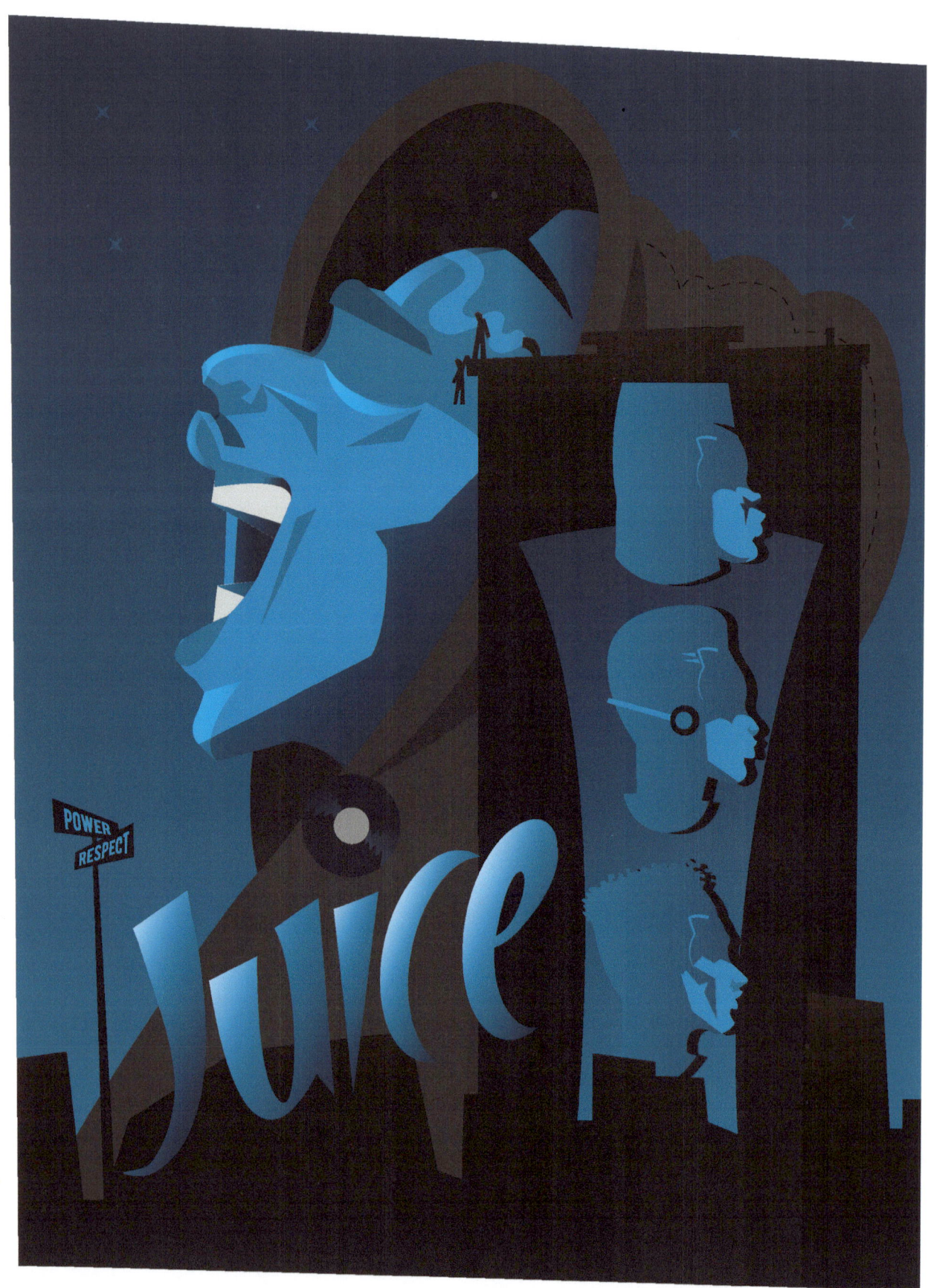

JUICE

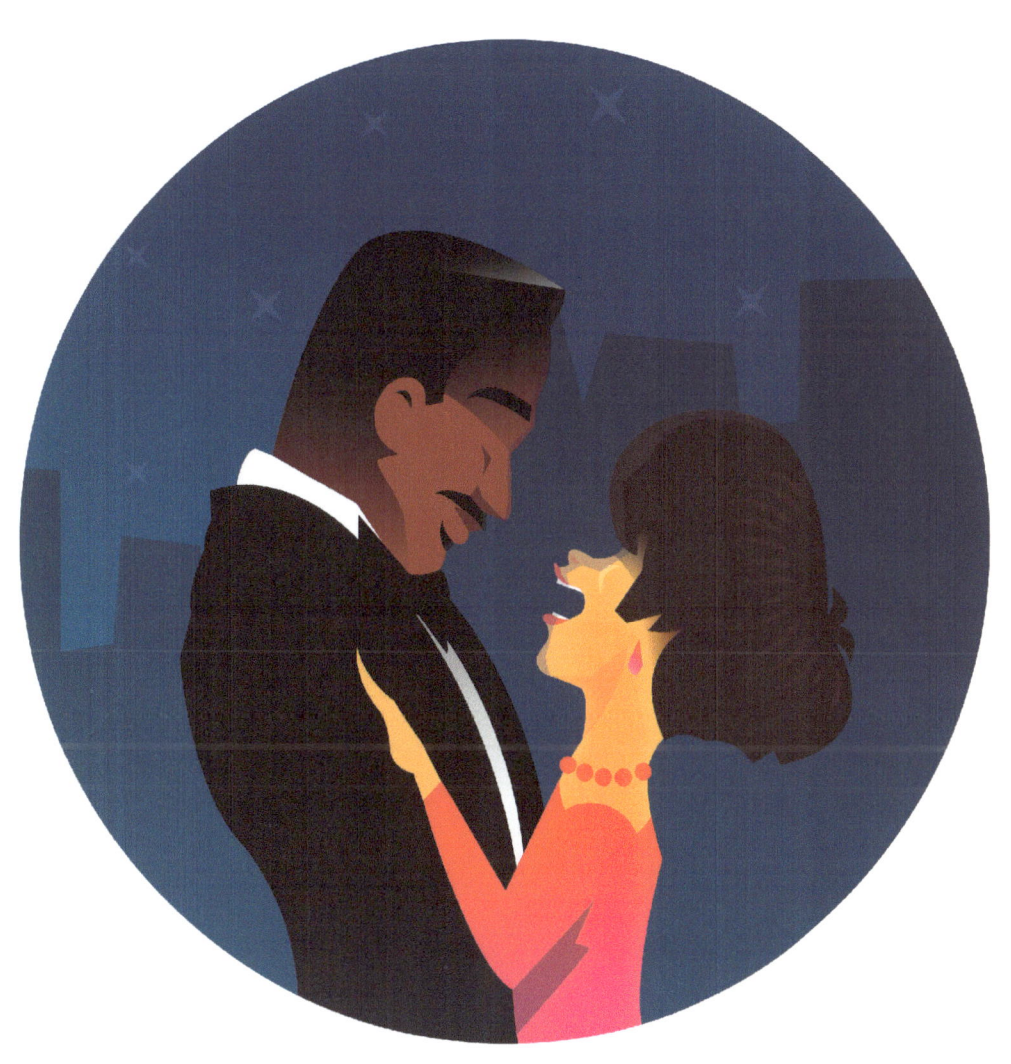

BOOMERANG

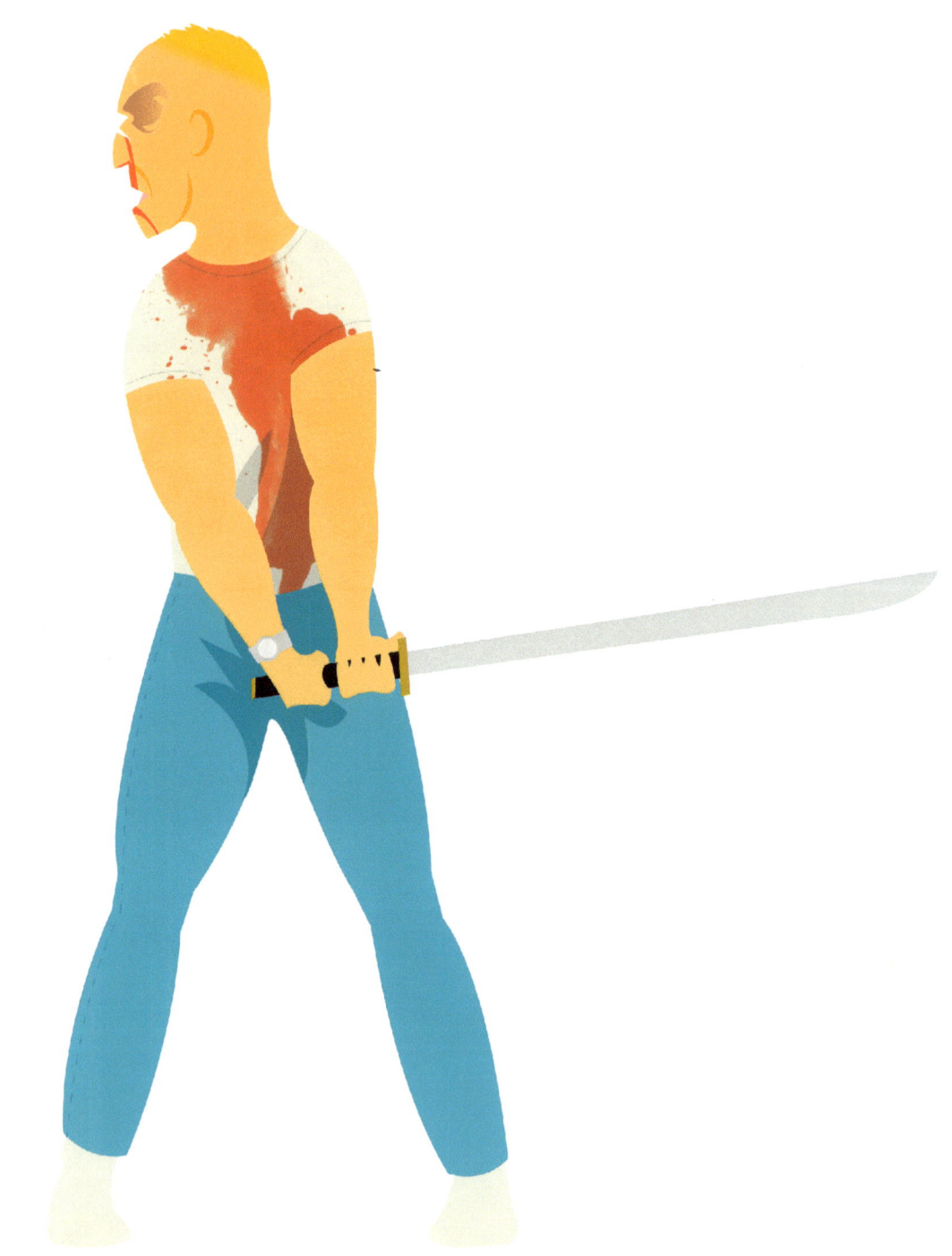

BUTCH

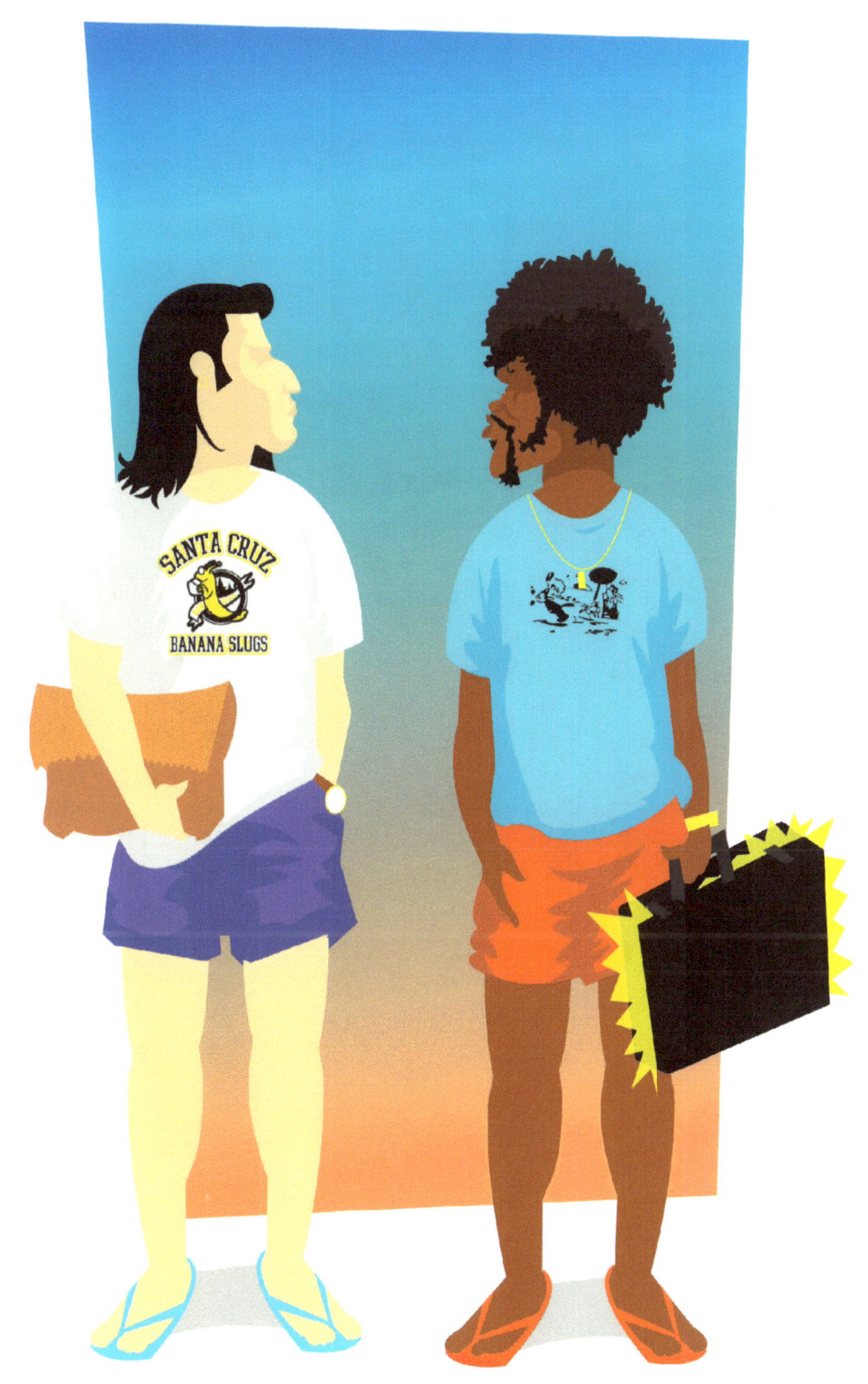

VINCENT AND JULES

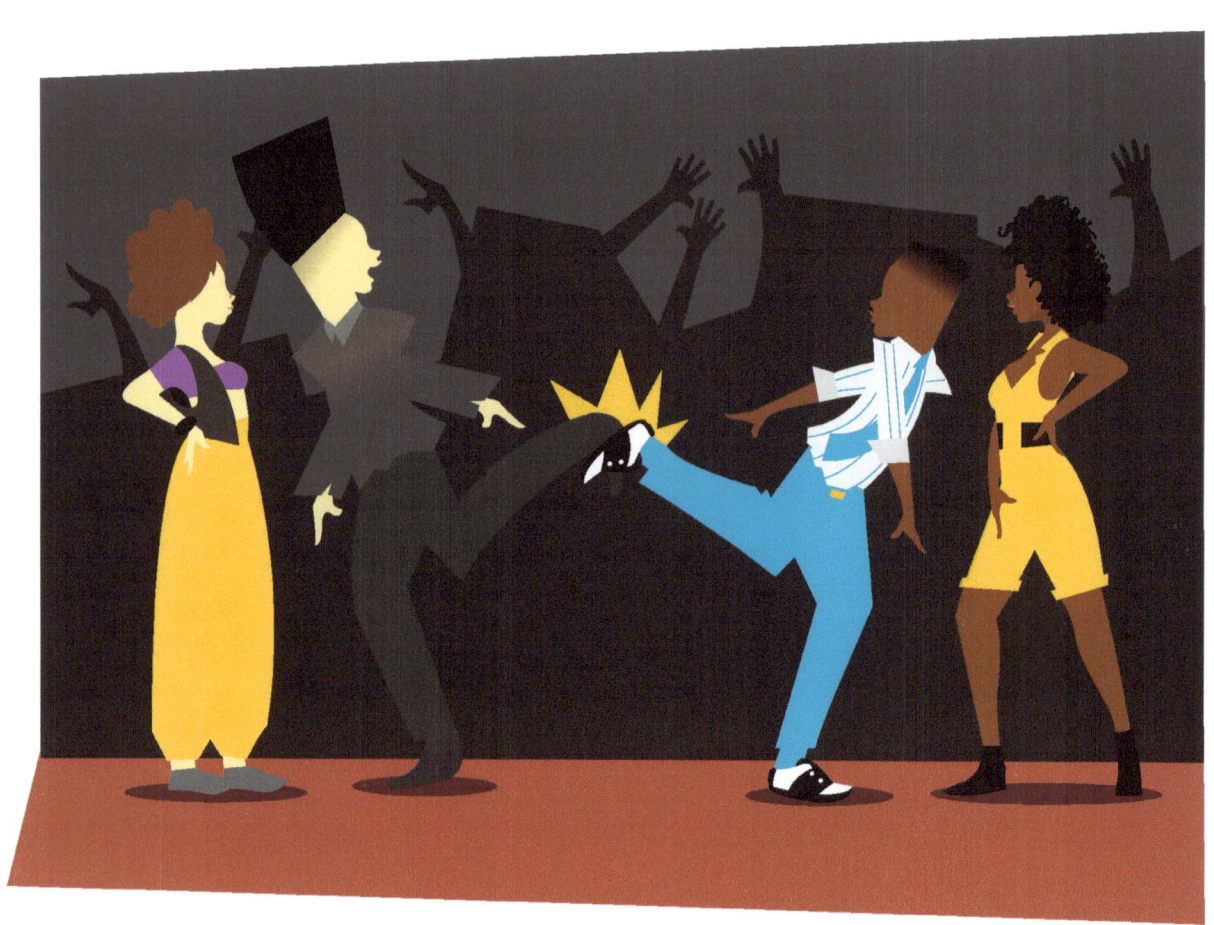

HOUSE PARTY

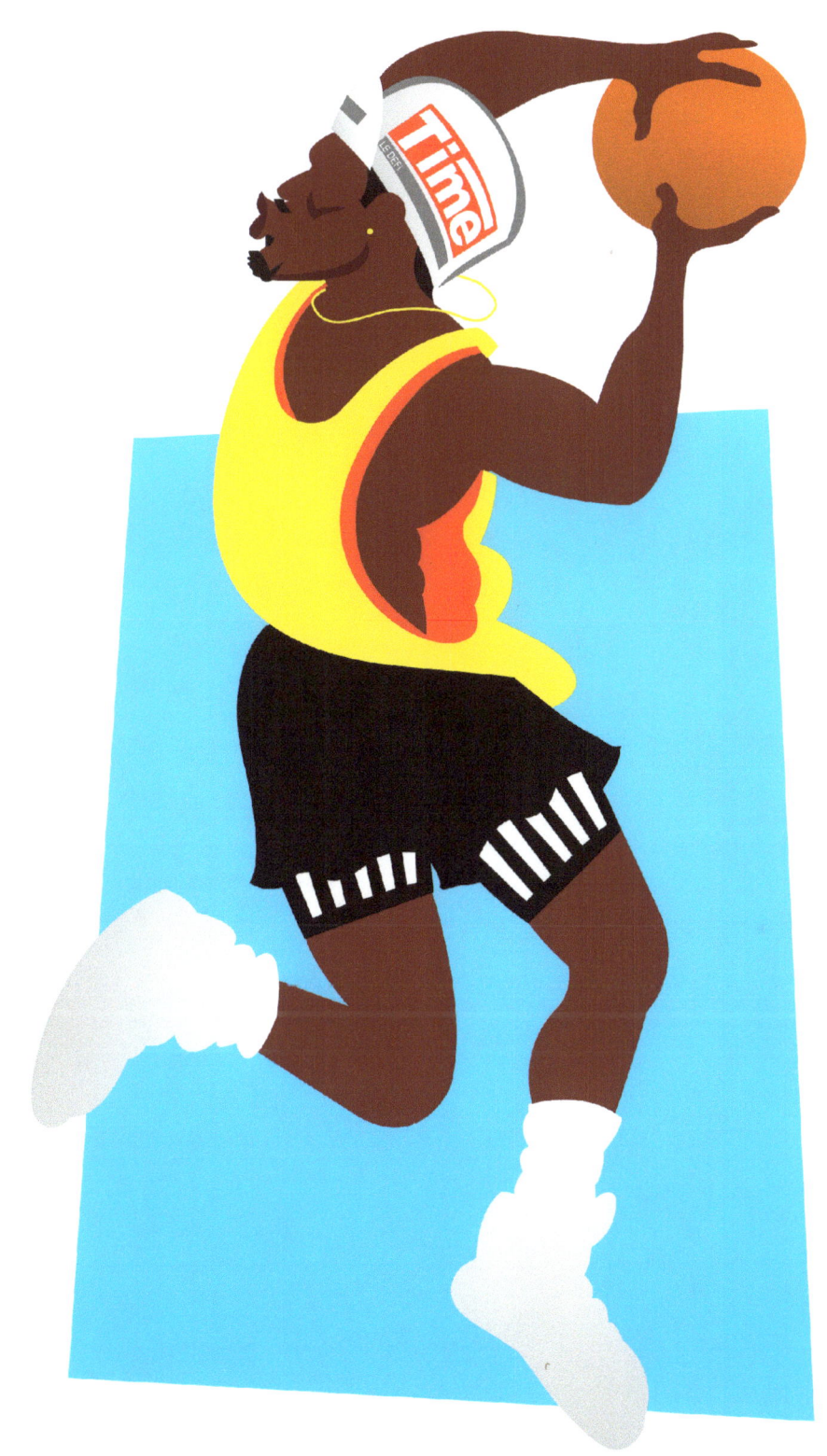

SIDNEY DEANE

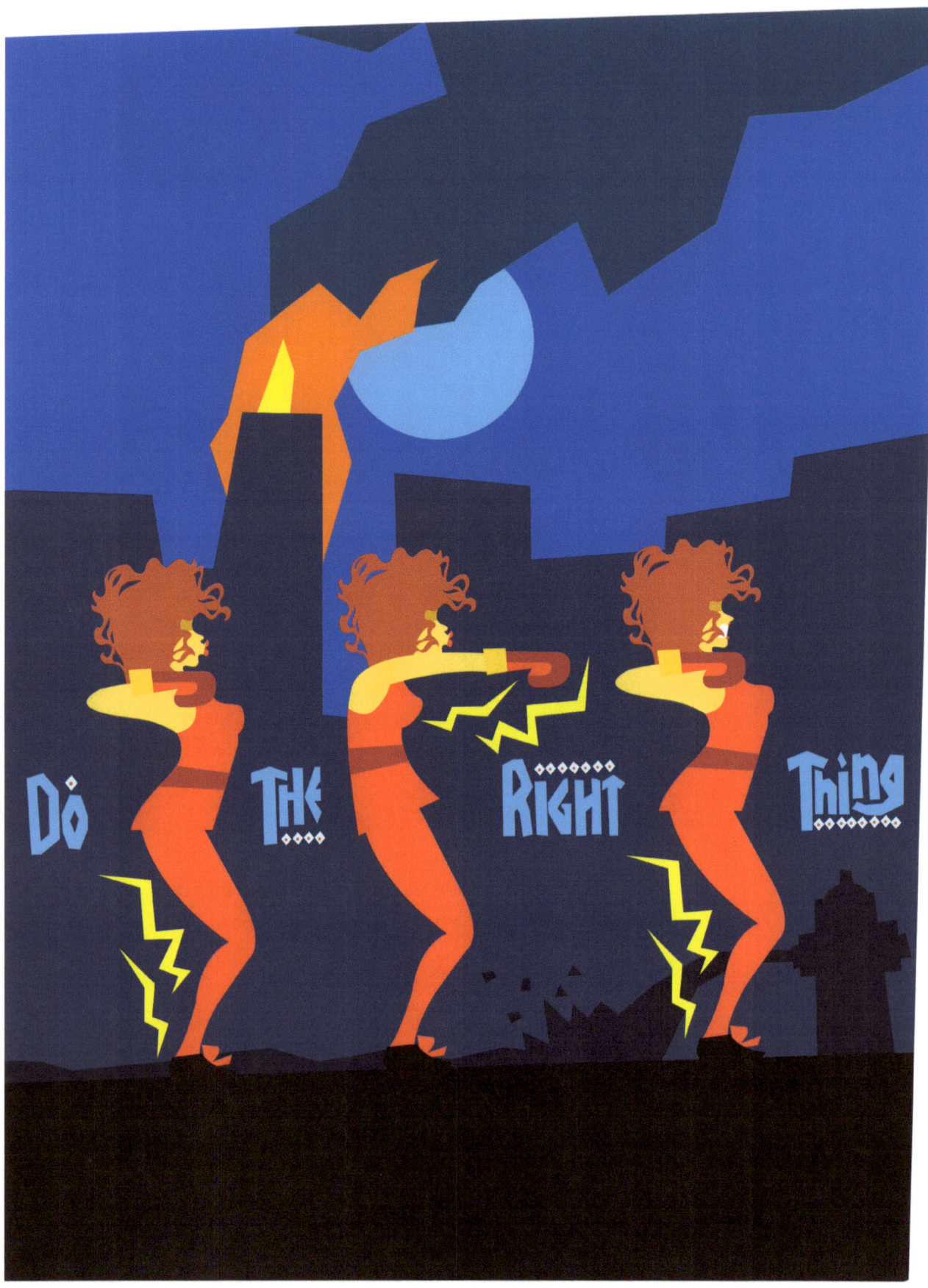

DO THE RIGHT THING

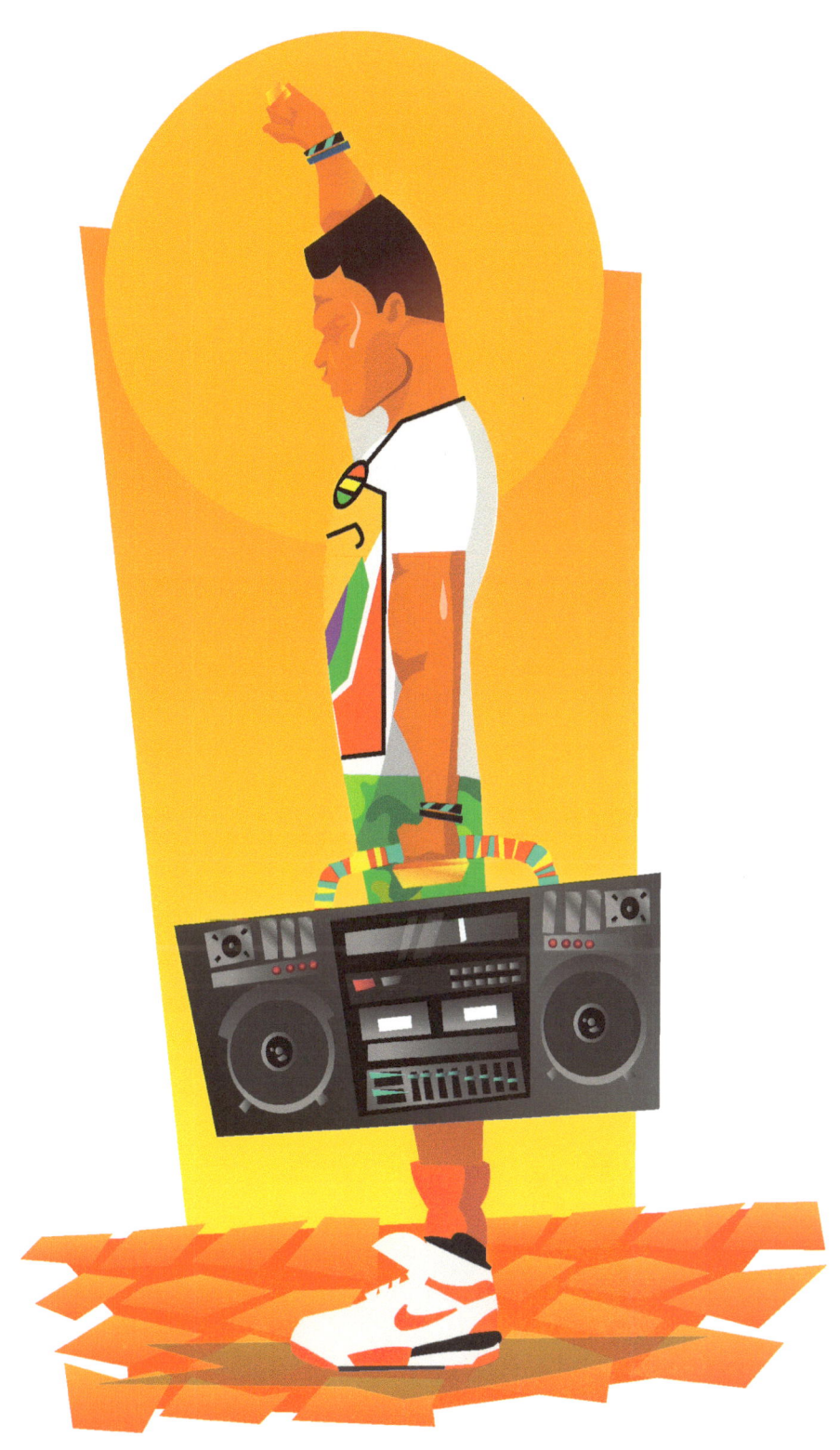

RADIO RAHEEM

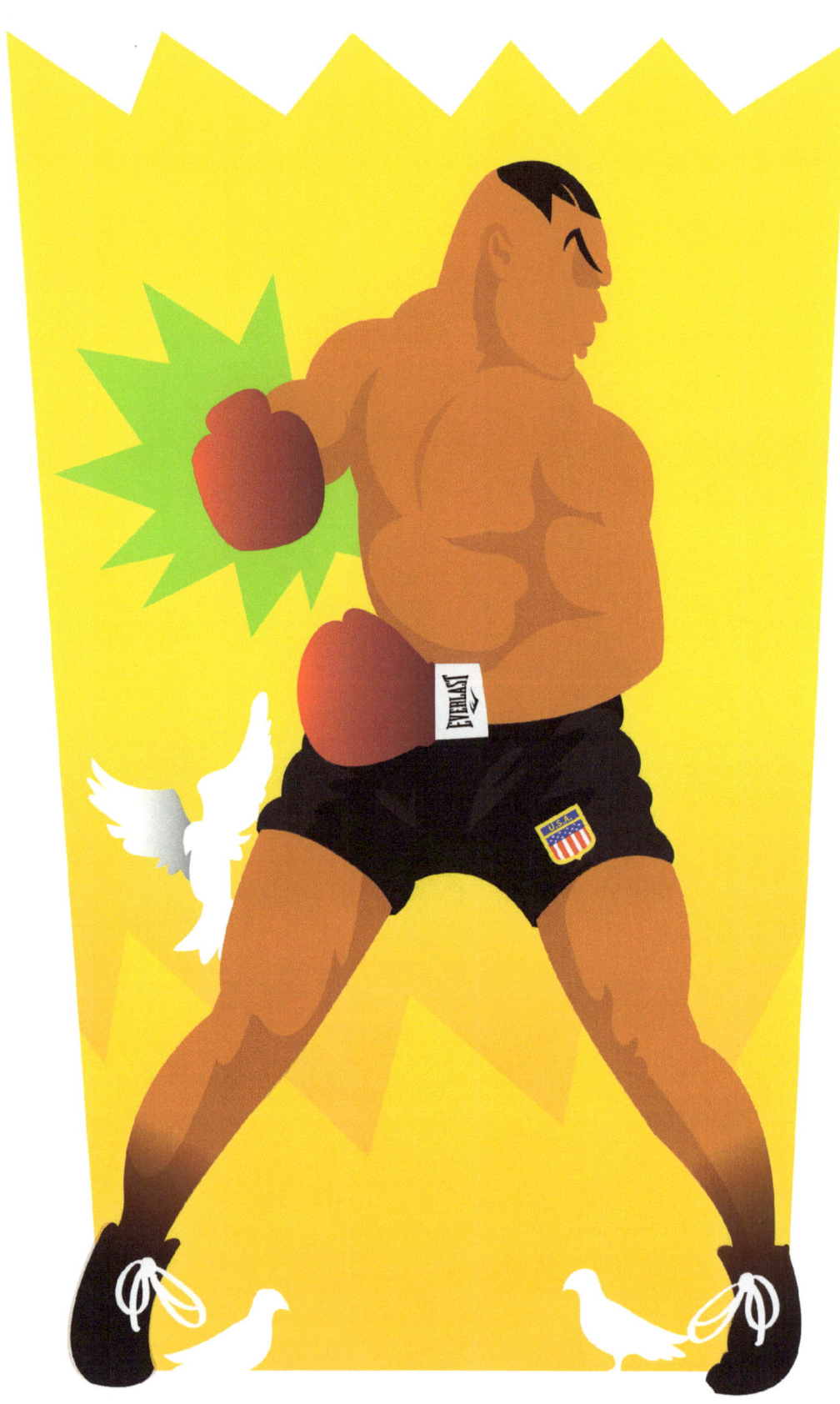

Mike Tyson

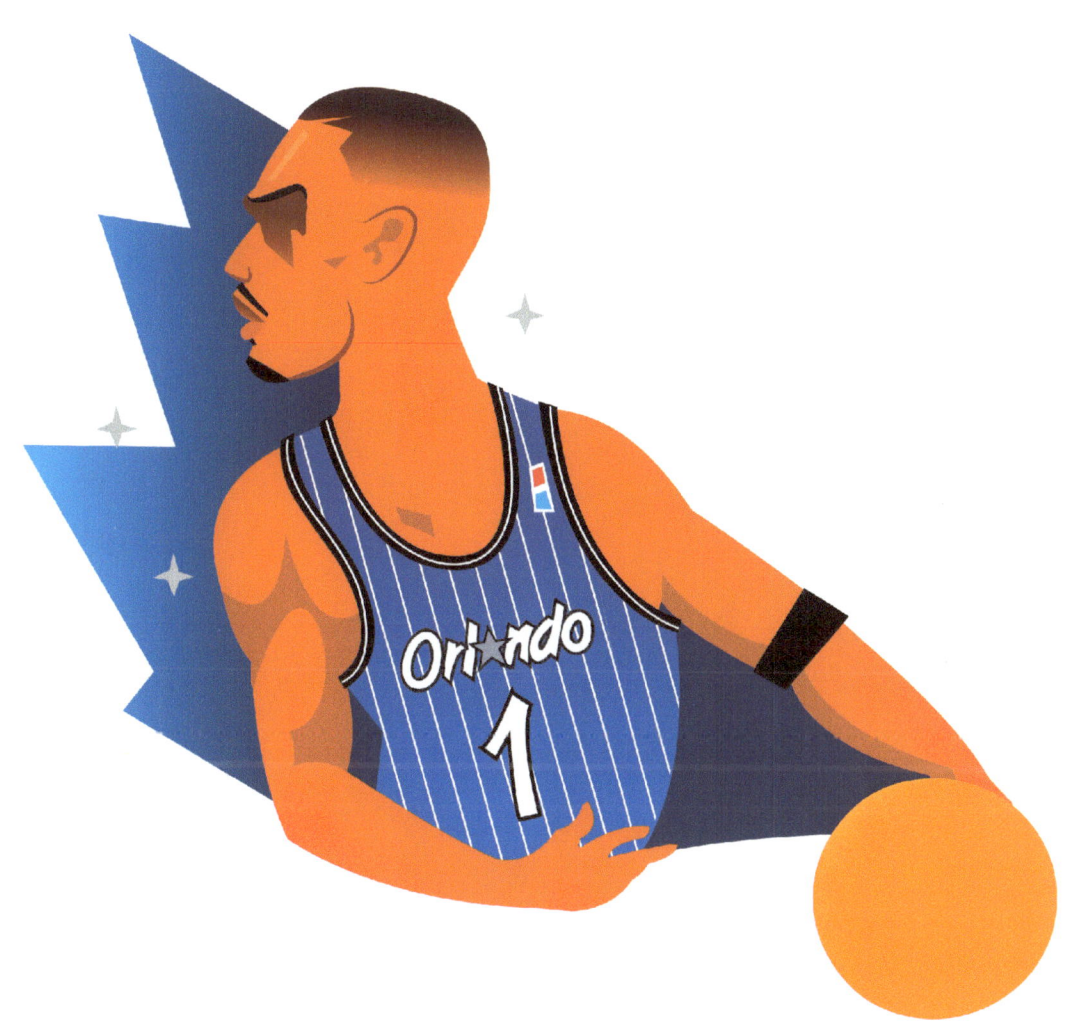

PENNY

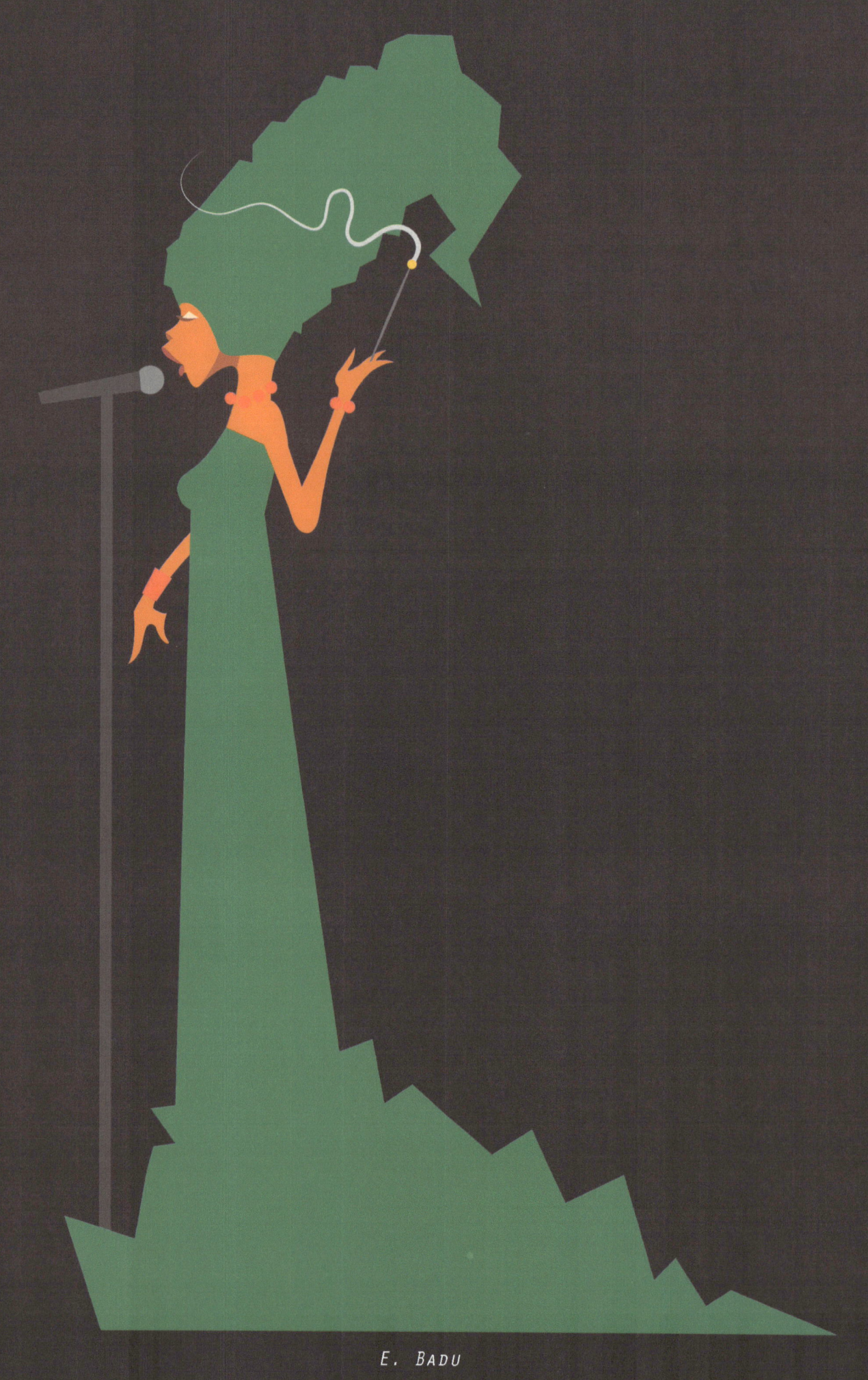

E. BADU

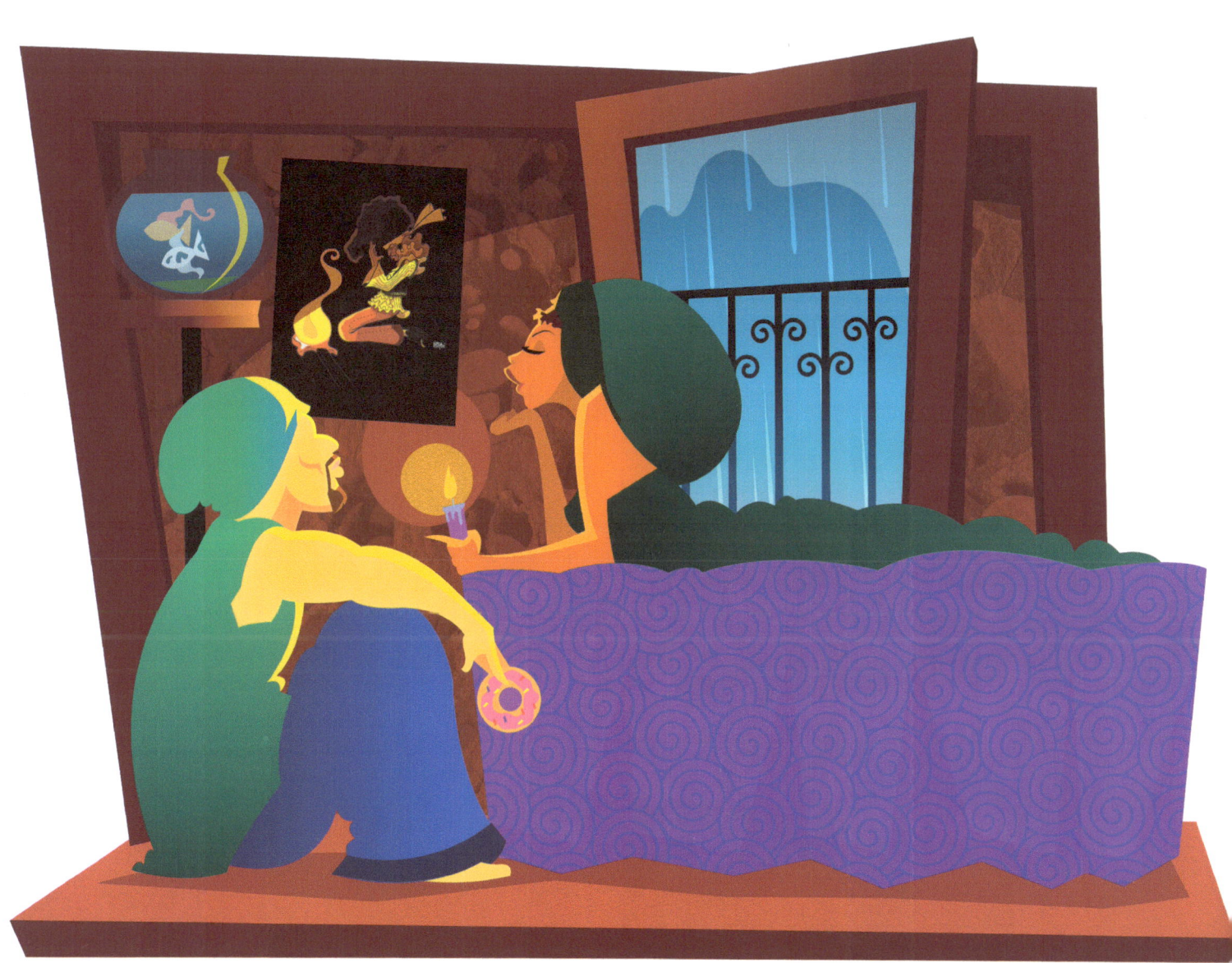

THE LIGHT

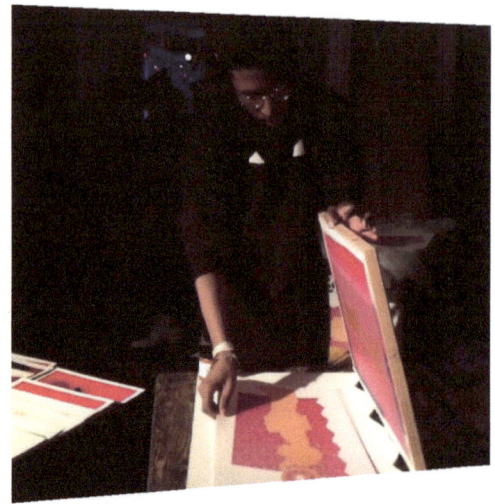

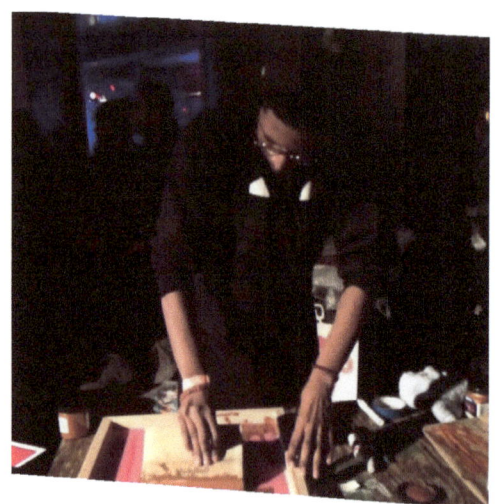

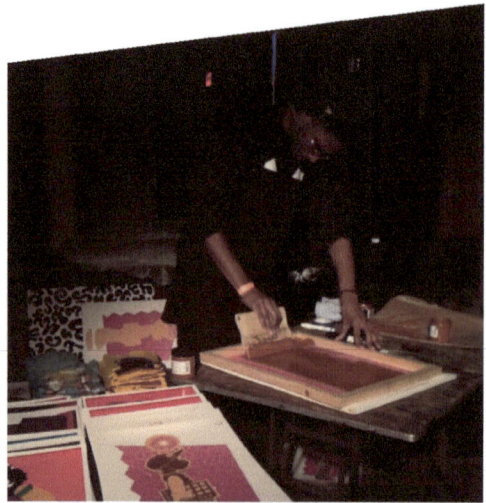

j_en_v   ⏱ 16w

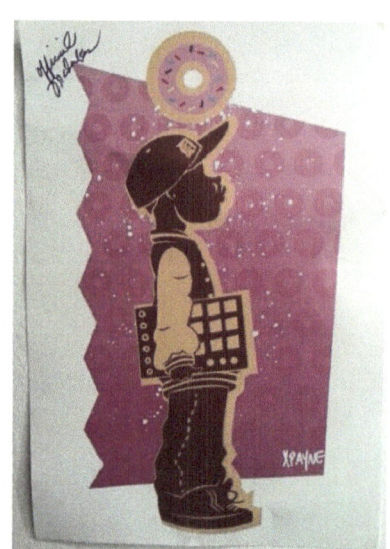

♥ **45 likes**

j_en_v Official... Art work by @xpayneart. Signed by the one and only, J. Dilla's mom, "Ma Dukes" #xpayneart #art #dillasdonuts #officialmadukes

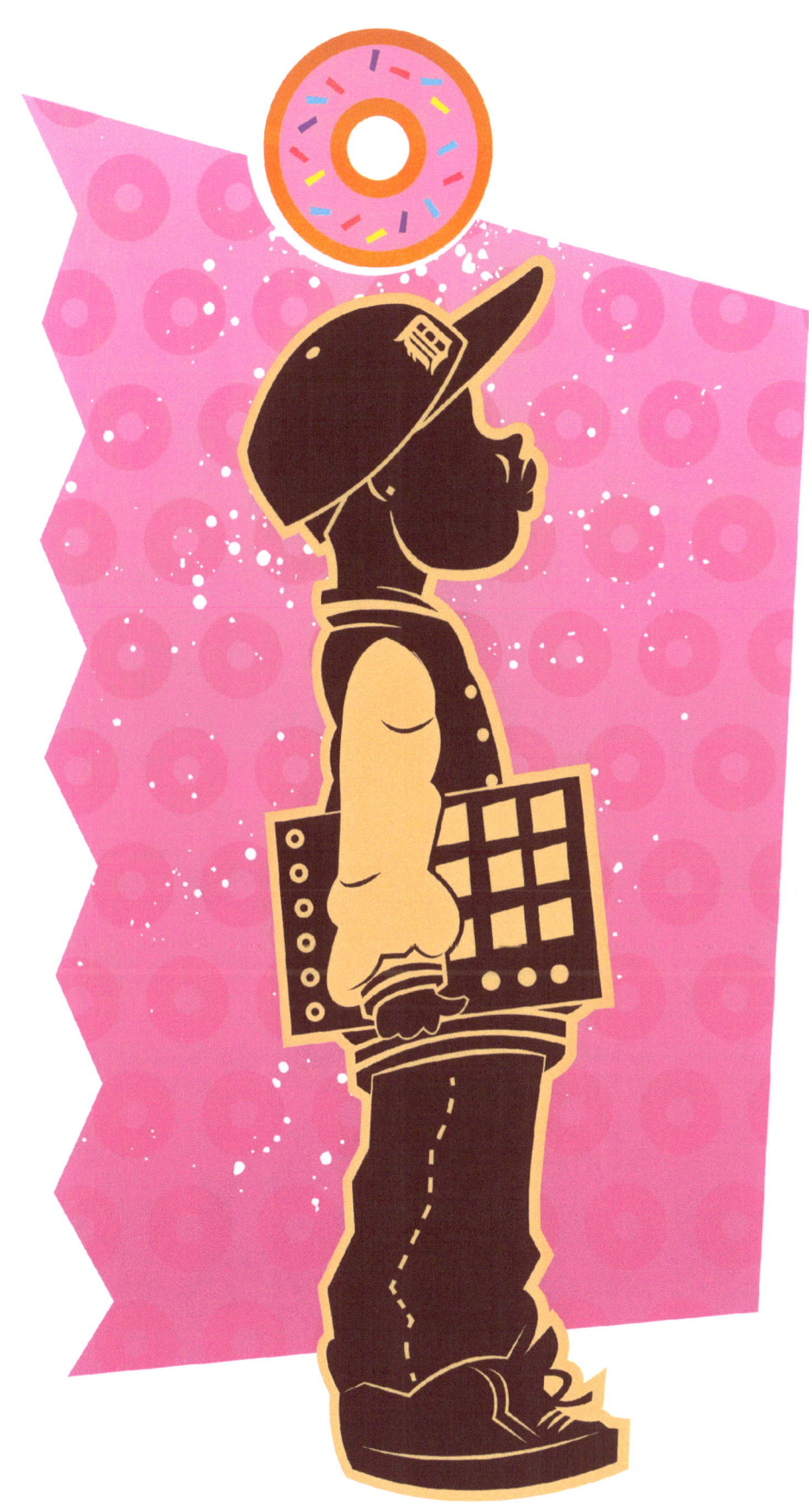

A LIL DILLA

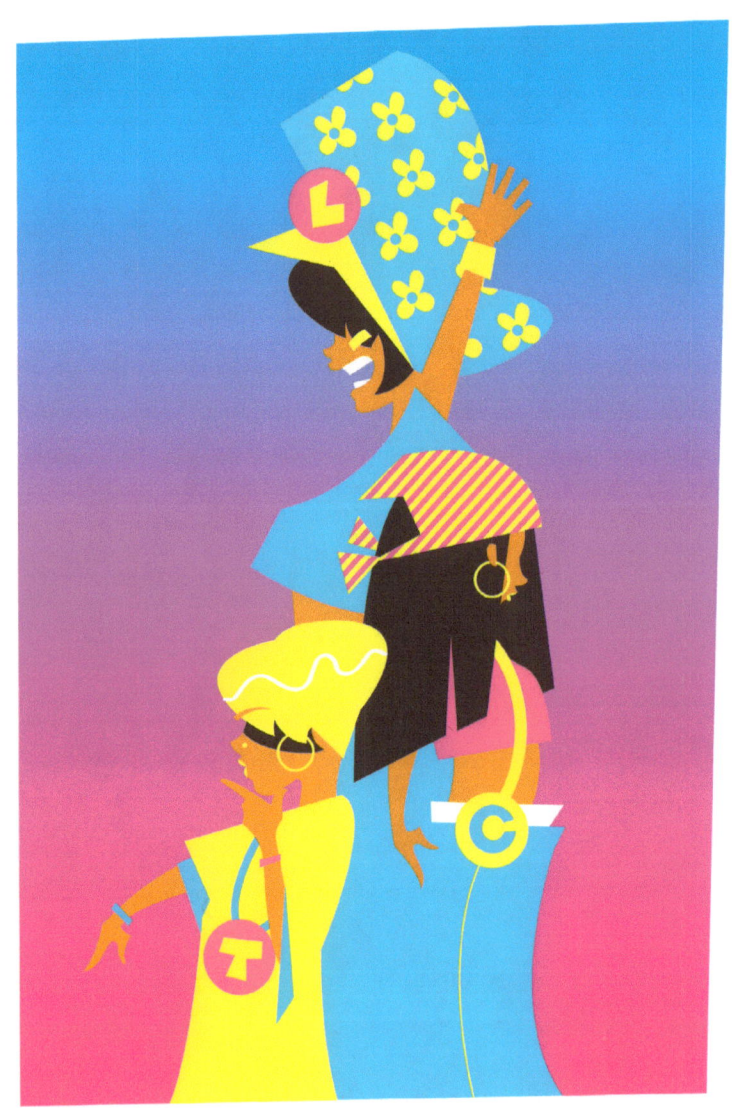

TLC

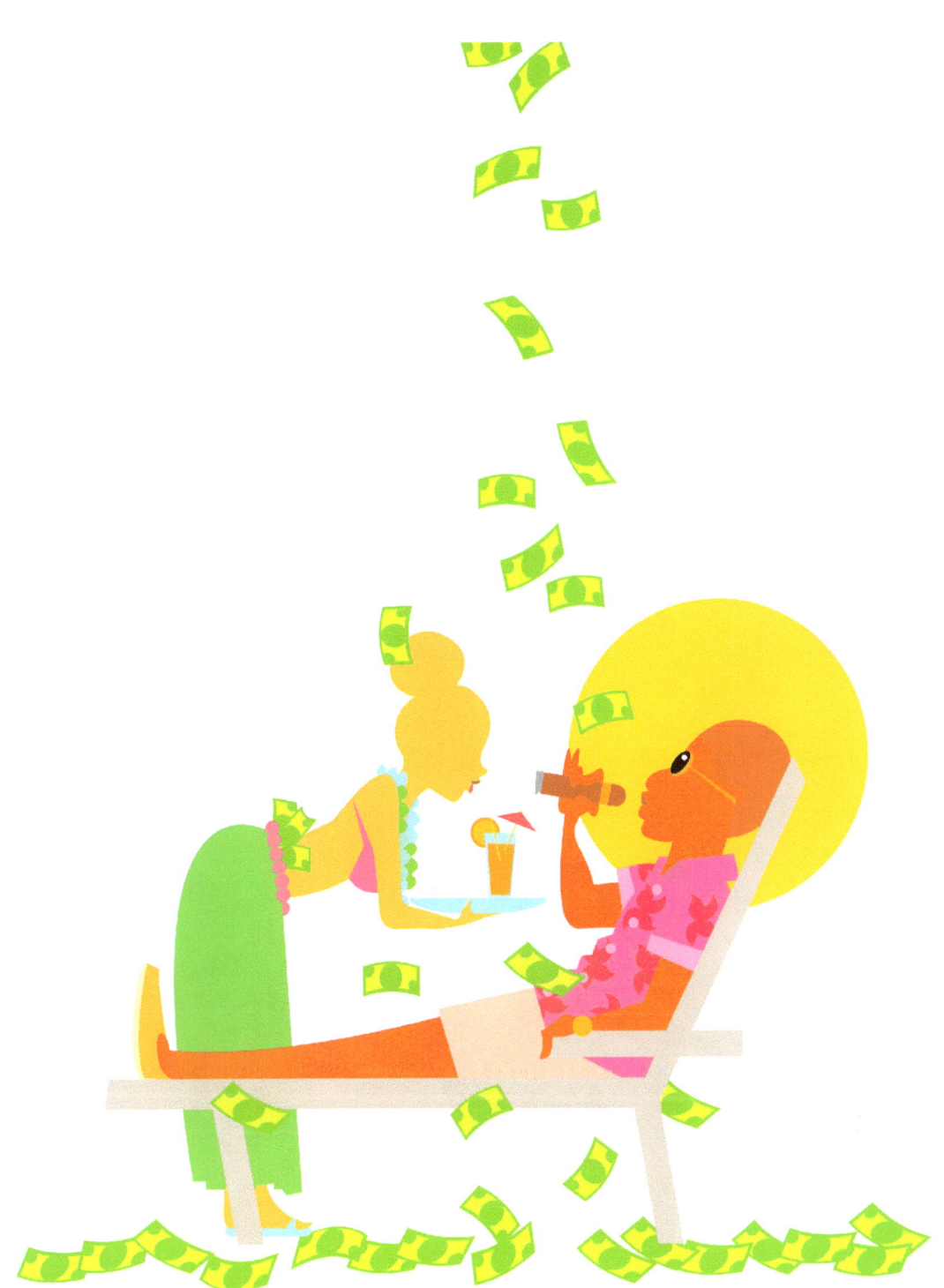

FEELIN' IT

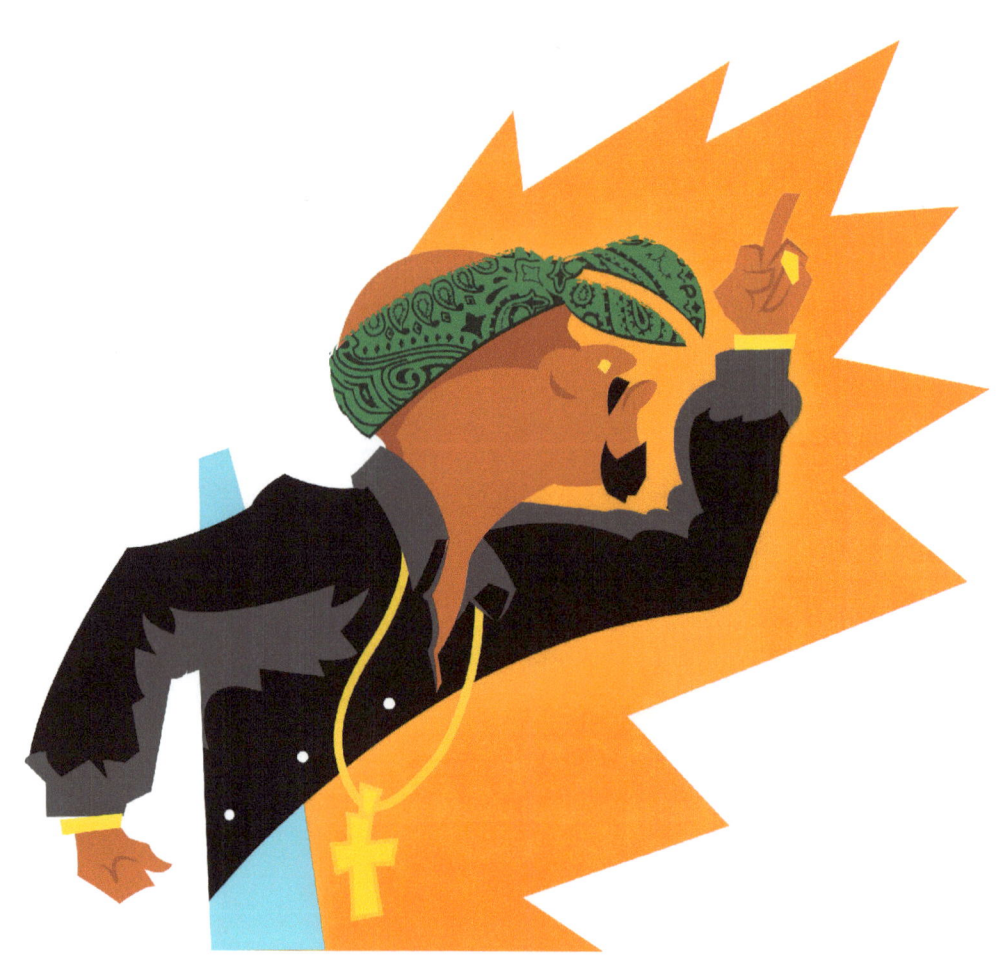

HIT 'EM UP

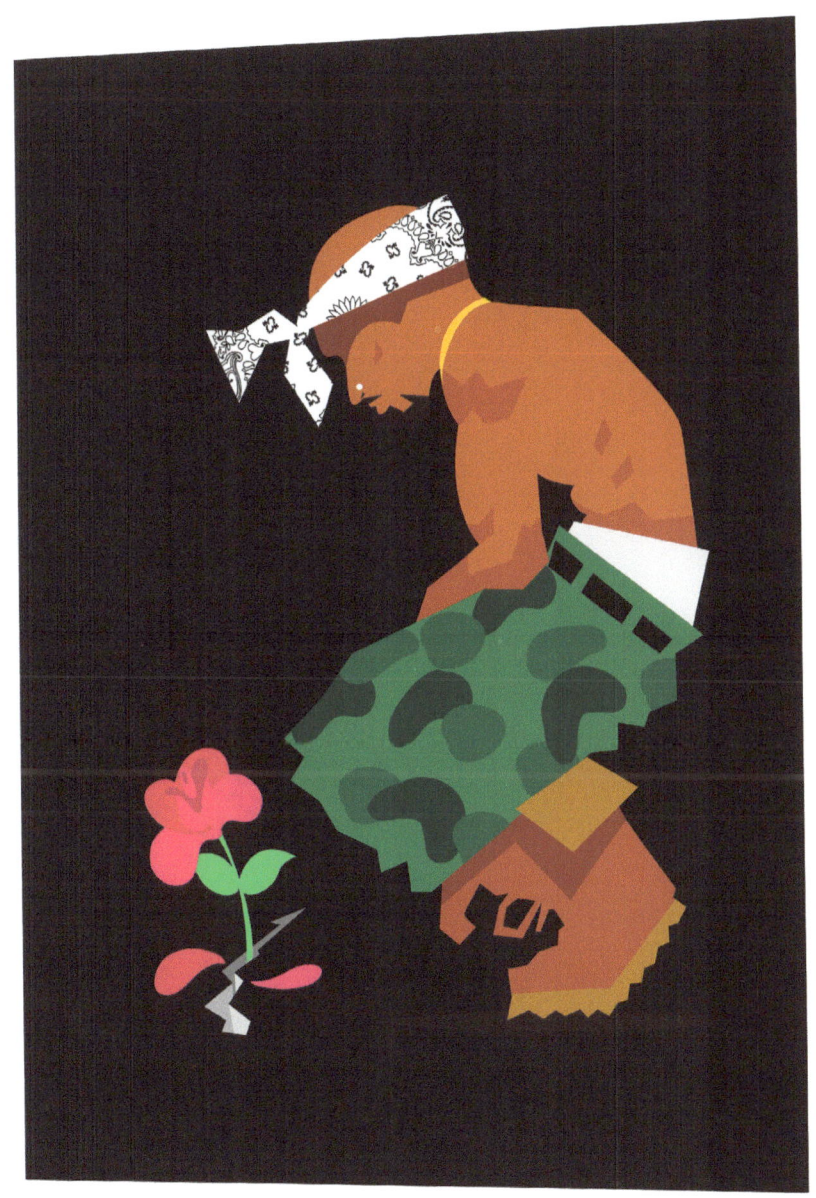

CONCRETE ROSE

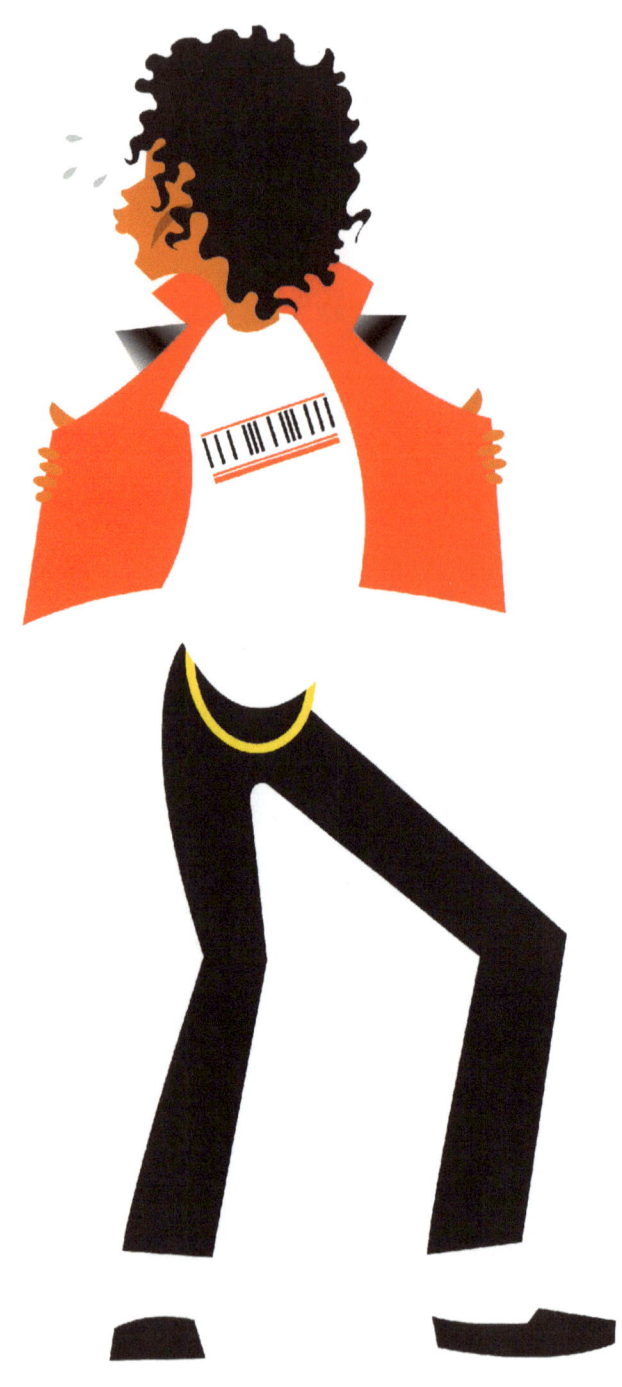

MJ

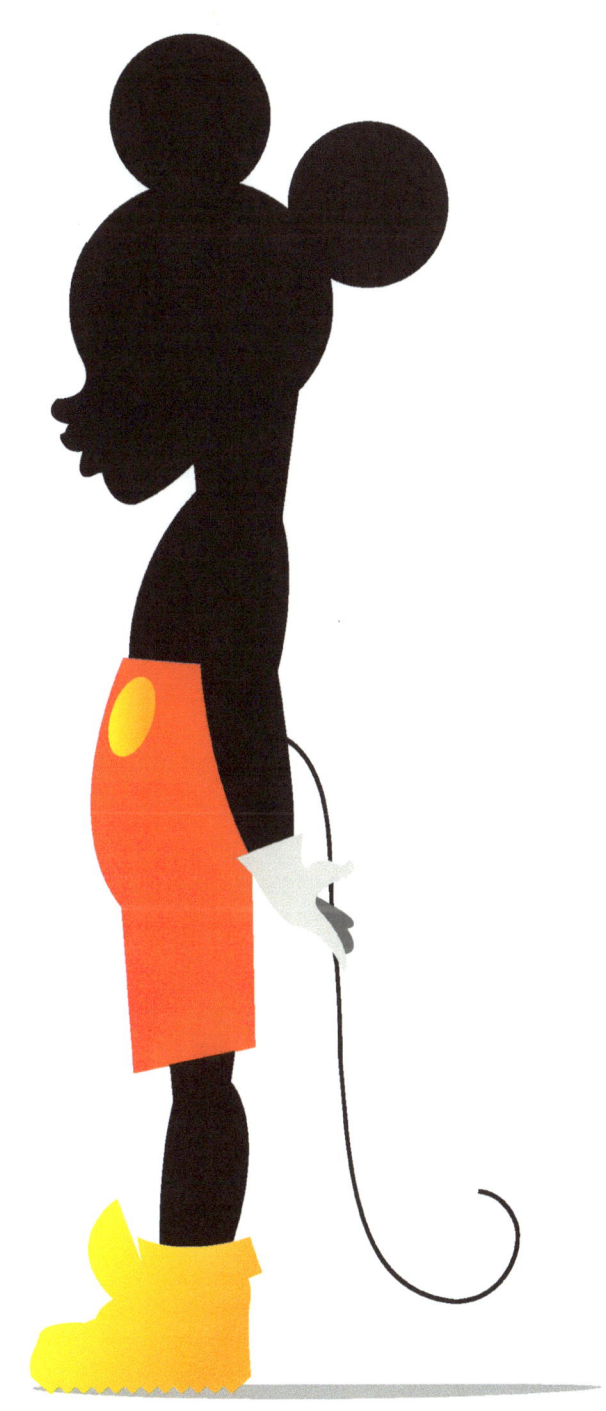

MICKEY

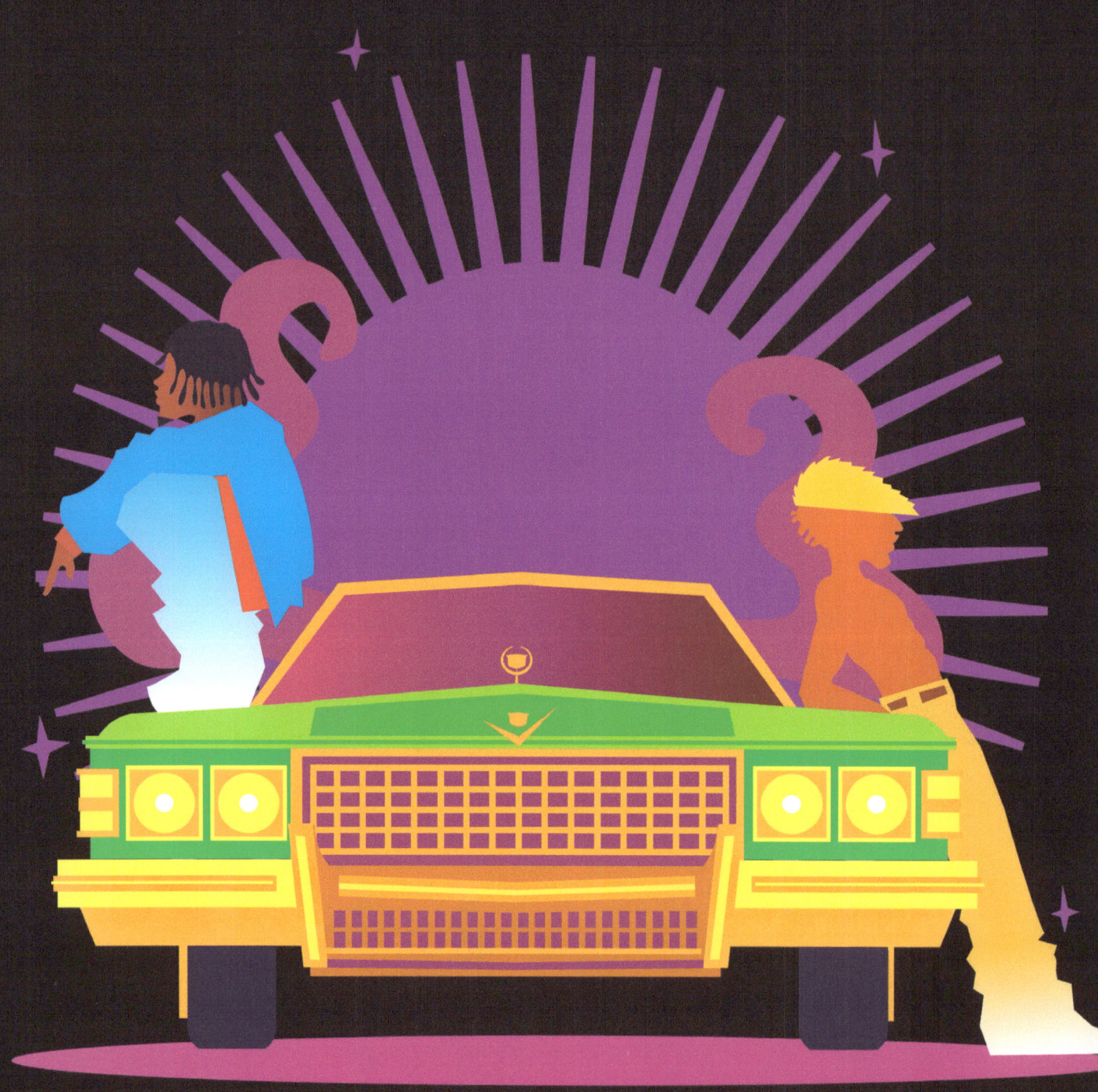

SOUTHERNPLAYALISTICADILLACMUZIK

SOUTHERN PLAYAS

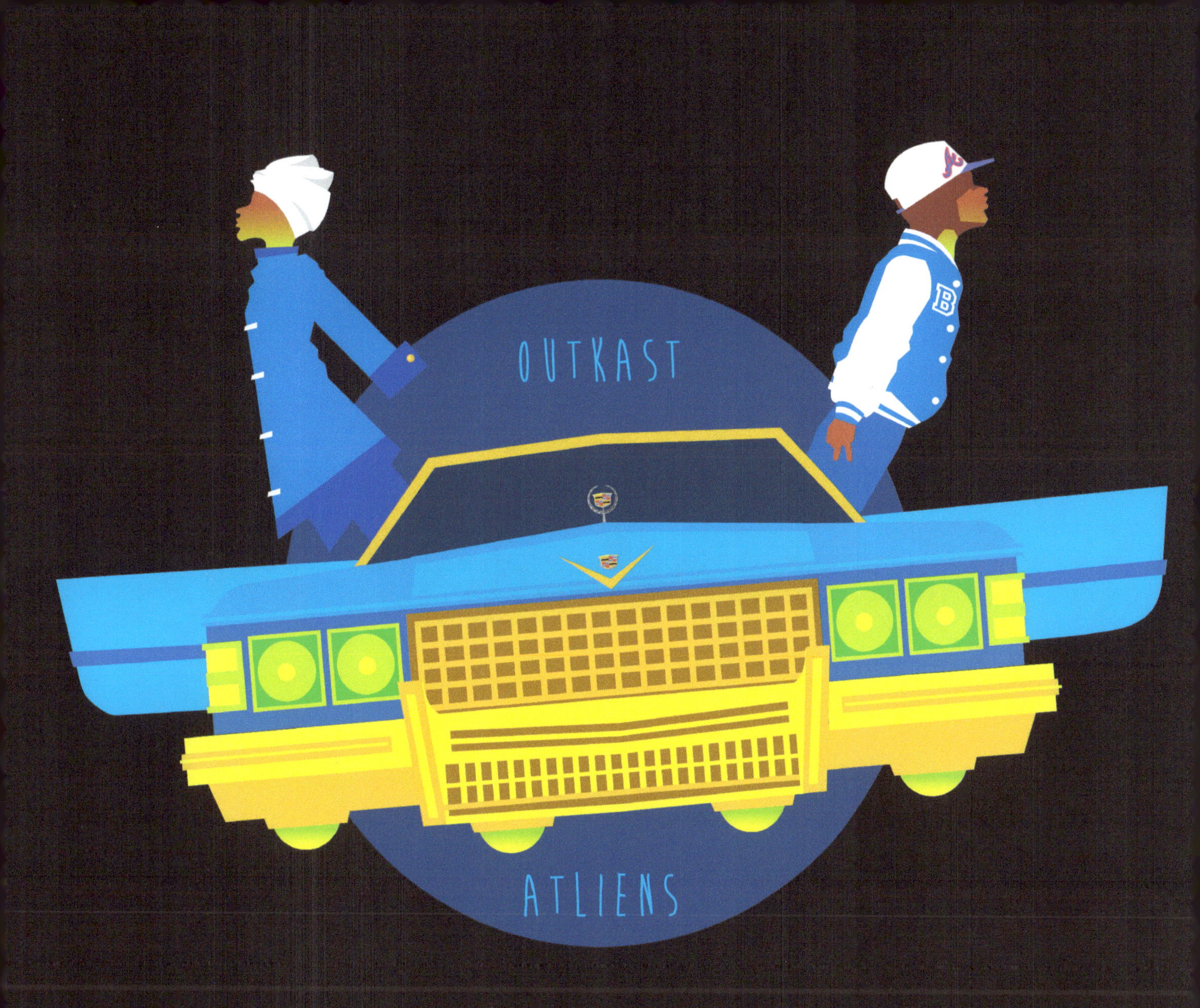

OUTKAST

ATLIENS

ATLIENS

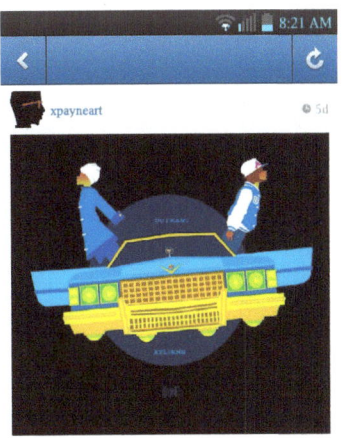

...AND I REPLIED I THAT I'VE BEEN GOING THROUGH THE SAME THINGS THAT YOU HAVE. TRUE, I GOT MORE FANS THAN THE AVERAGE MAN BUT NOT ENOUGH LOOT LAST ME TO THE END OF THE WEEK I LIVE BY THE PIECE LIKE YOU LIVE CHECK TO CHECK. IF YOU DON'T TUMBLE ME THEN I DON'T EAT SO WE LIKE NECK TO NECK. GUESS I DONE COME A LONG WAY LIKE THOSE SLIM ASS CIGARETTES, FROM VIRGINIA I CAN'T STOP SO IMMA JUST CONTINUE.

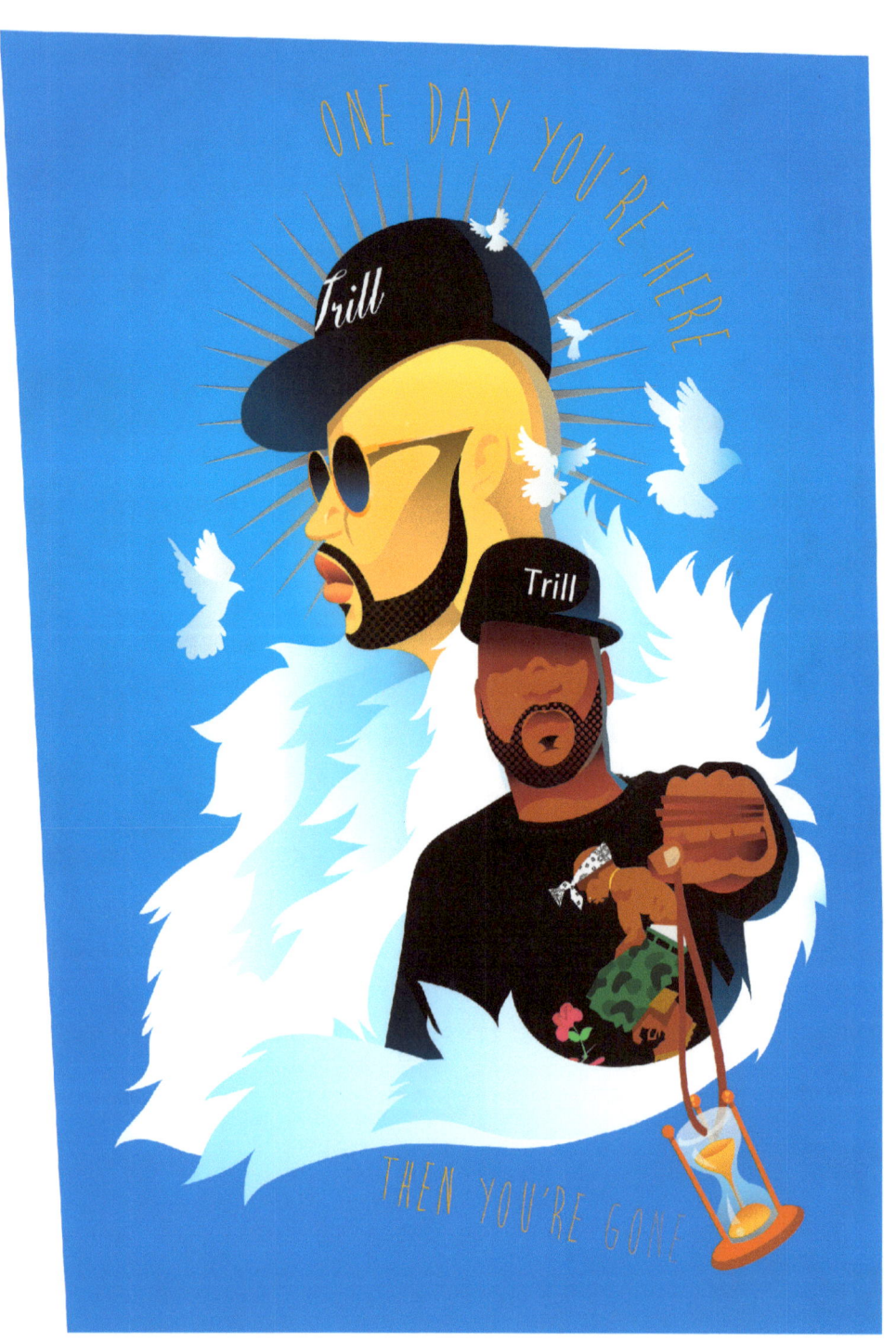

One Day You're Here

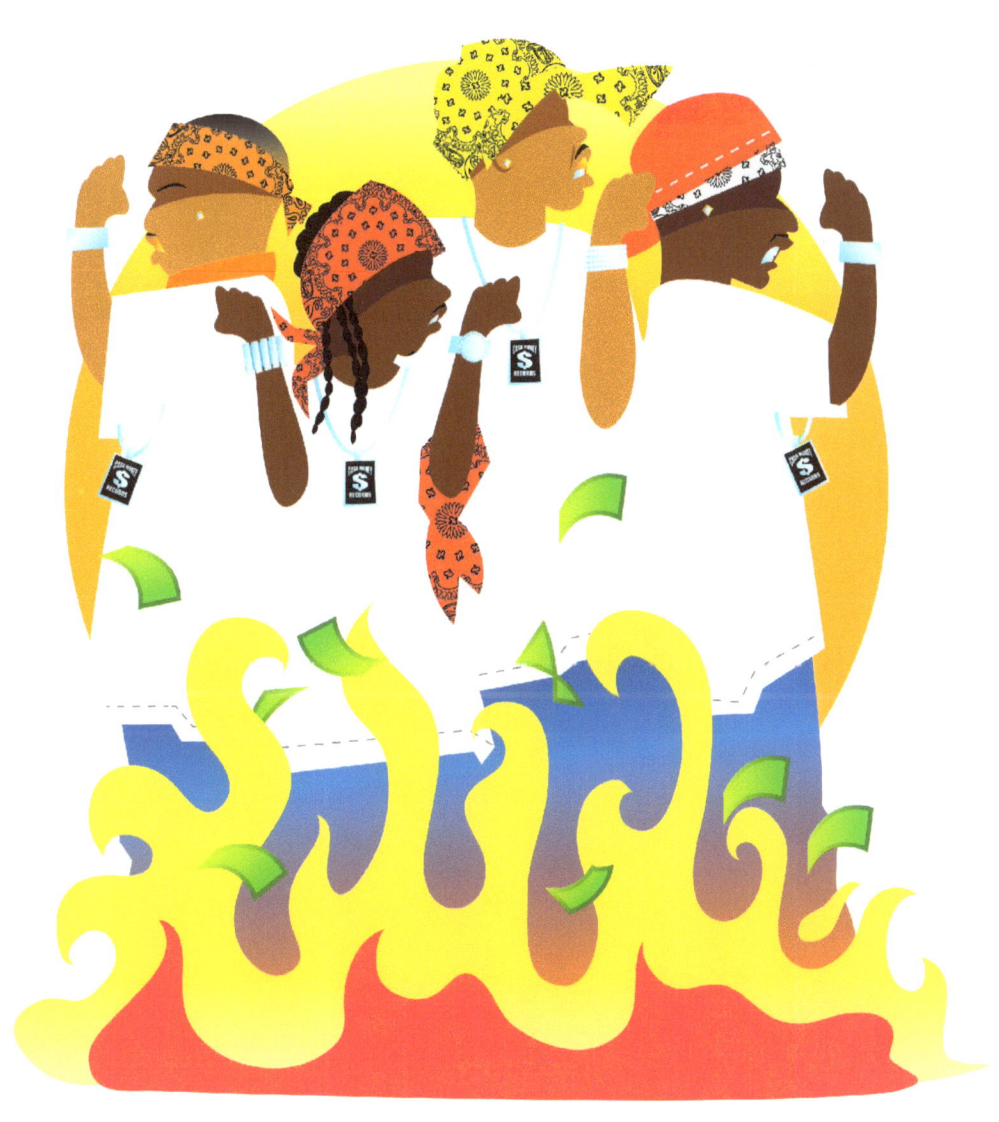

HOT BOYZ

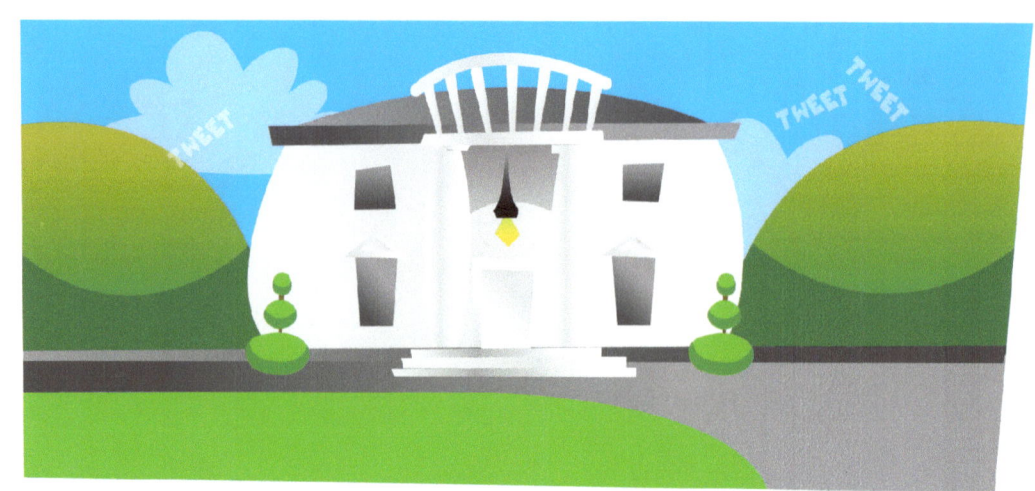

JAZZED

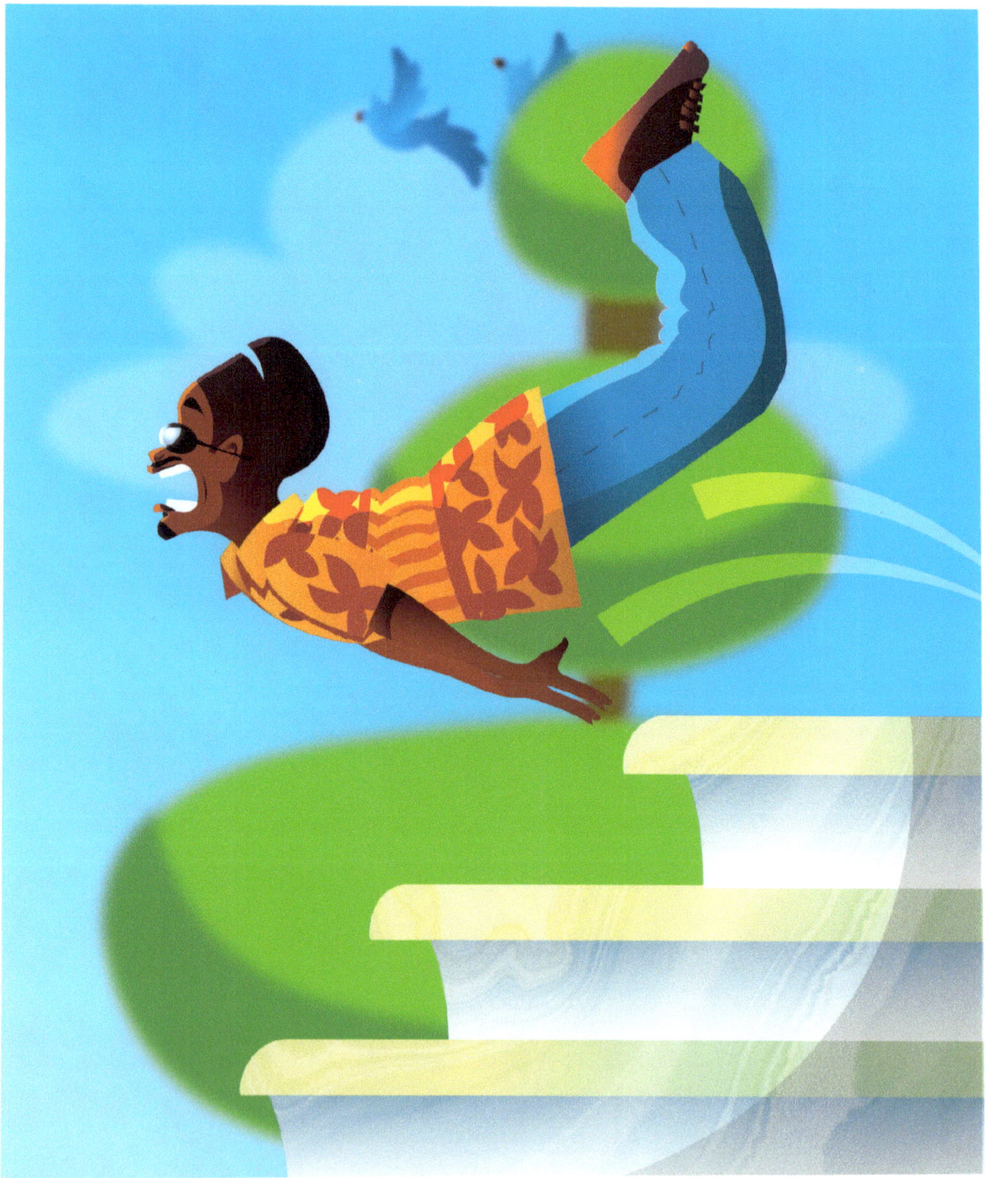

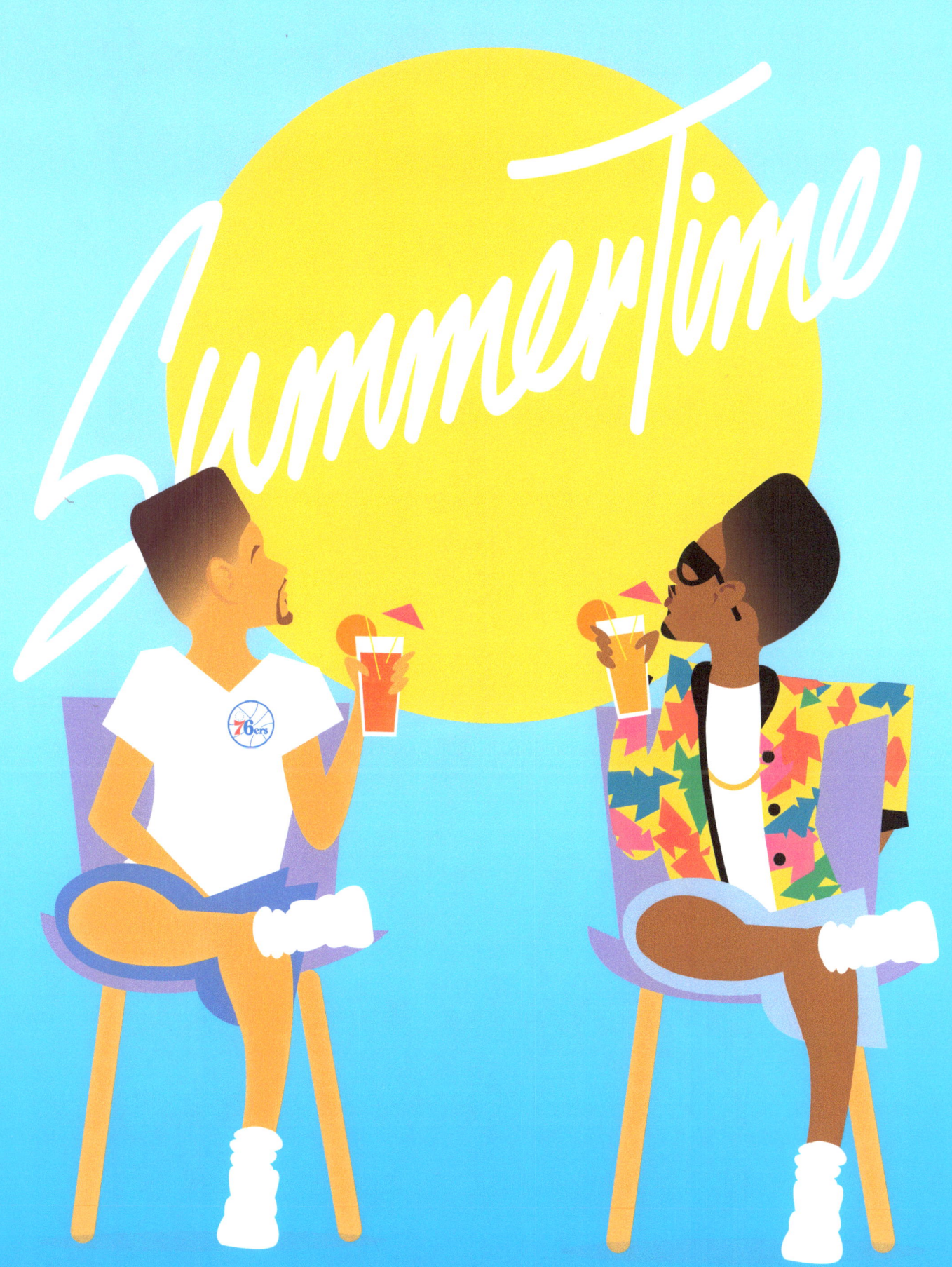

SUMMERTIME

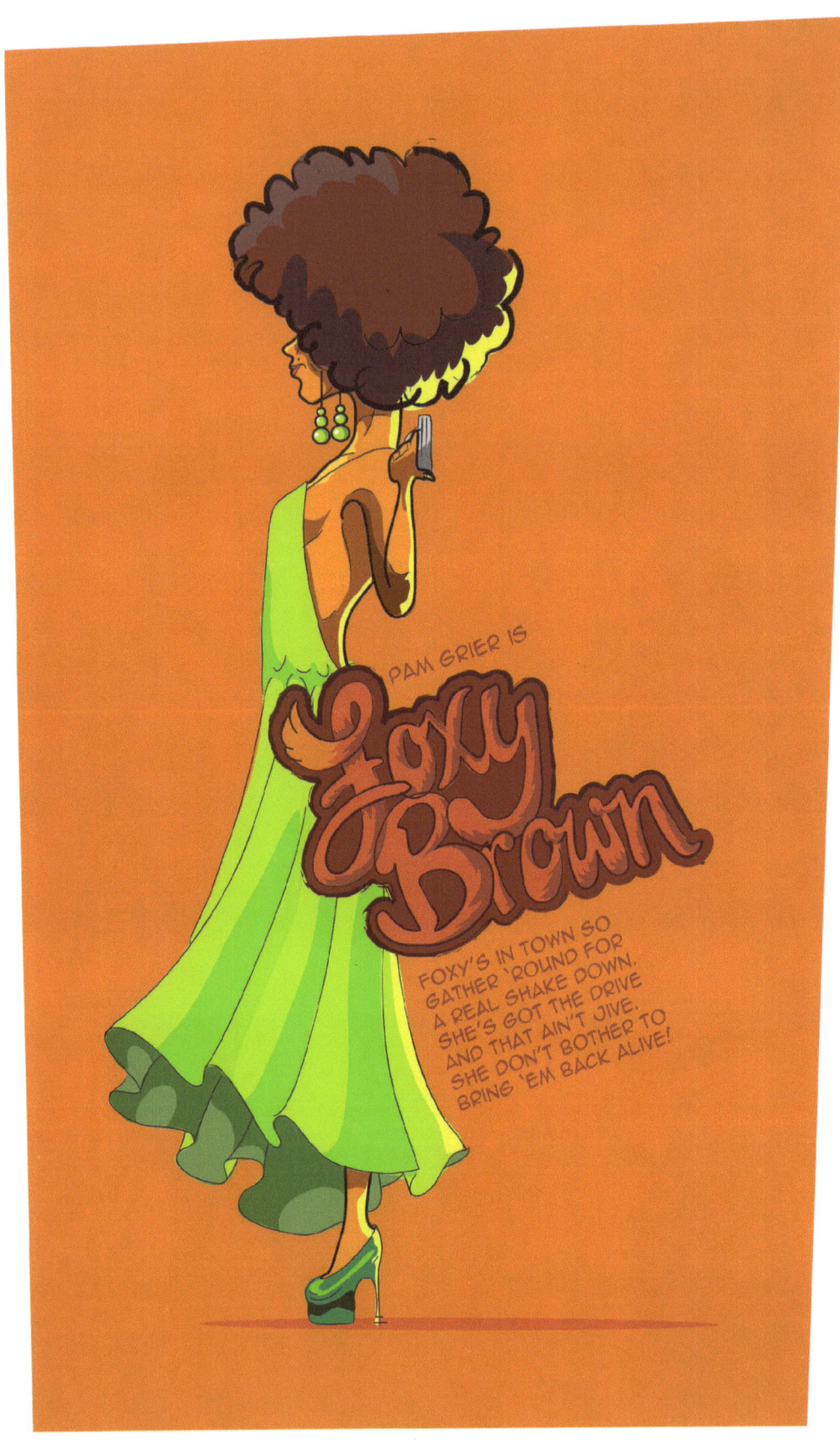

FOXY BROWN

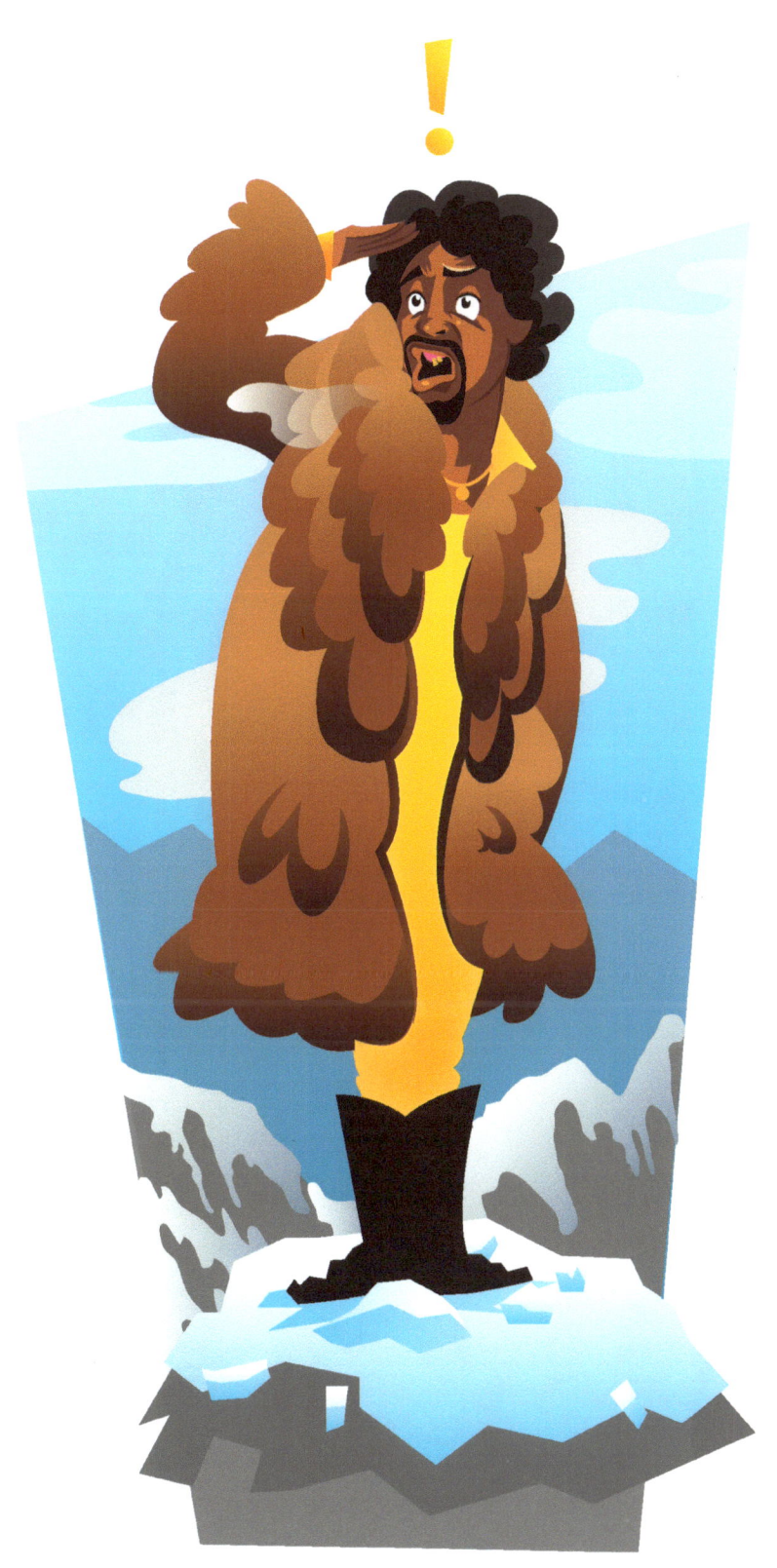

THE ORIGNAL PLAYER

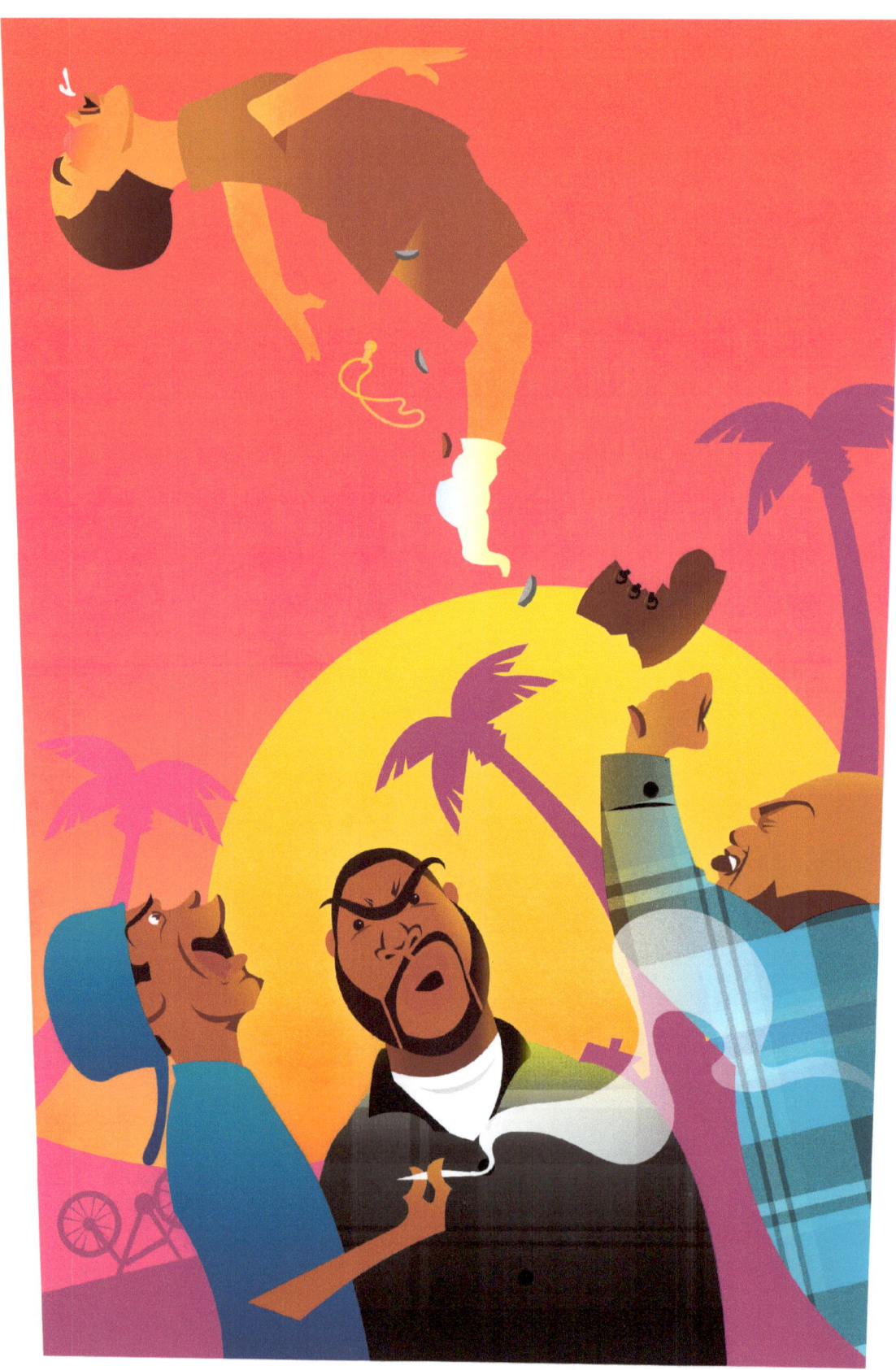

FRIDAY

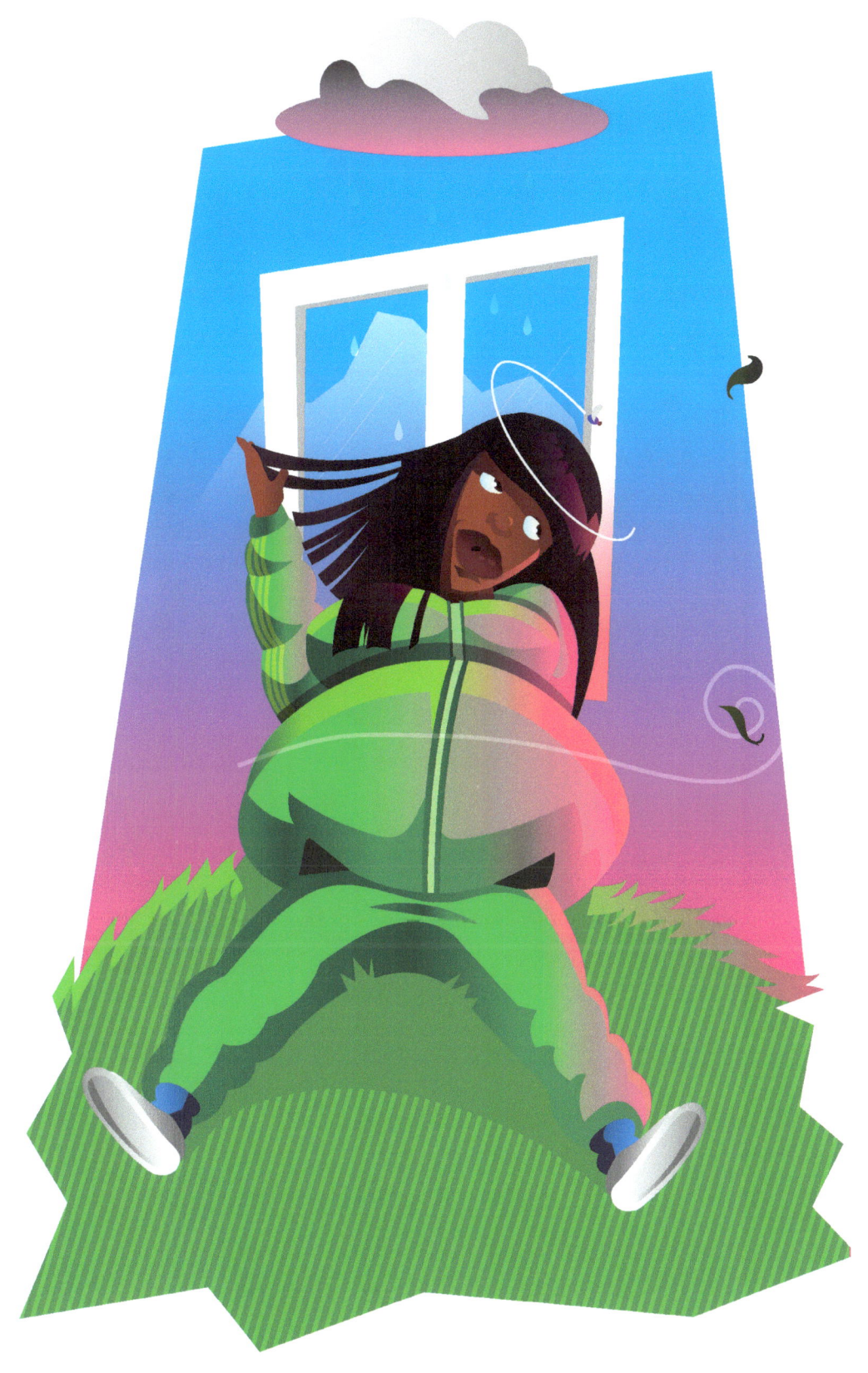

The Rain

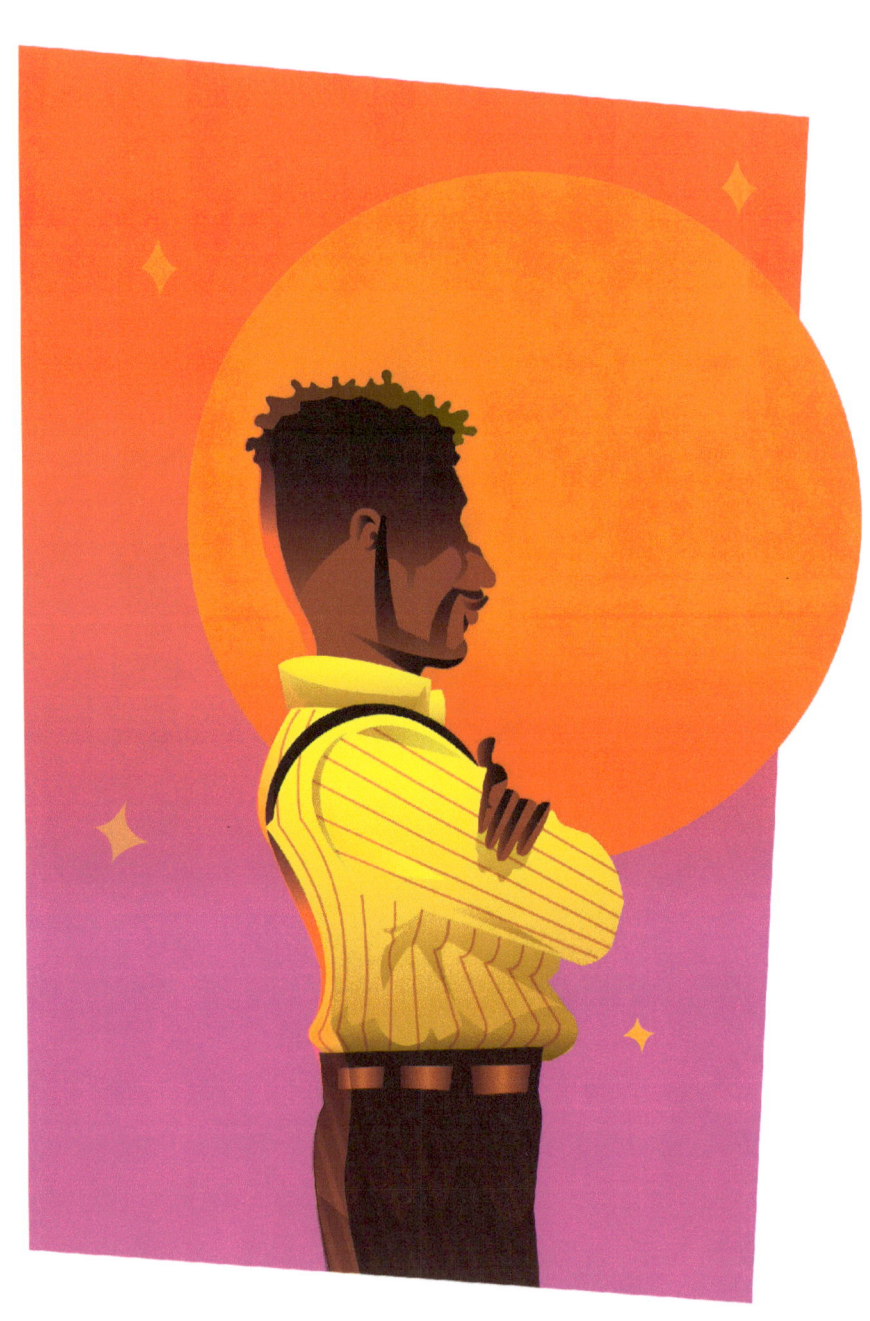

KYLE

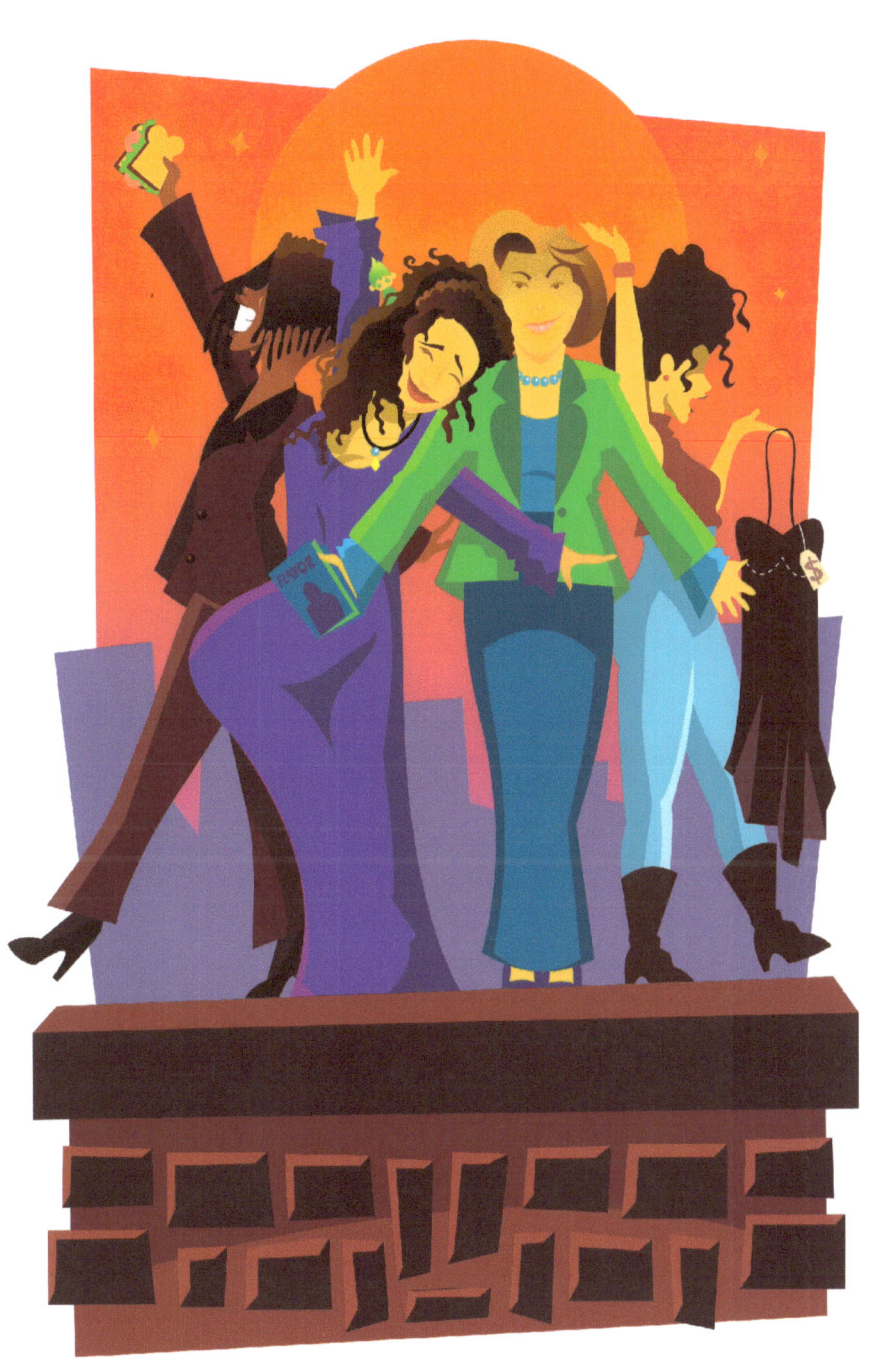

LIVING SINGLE

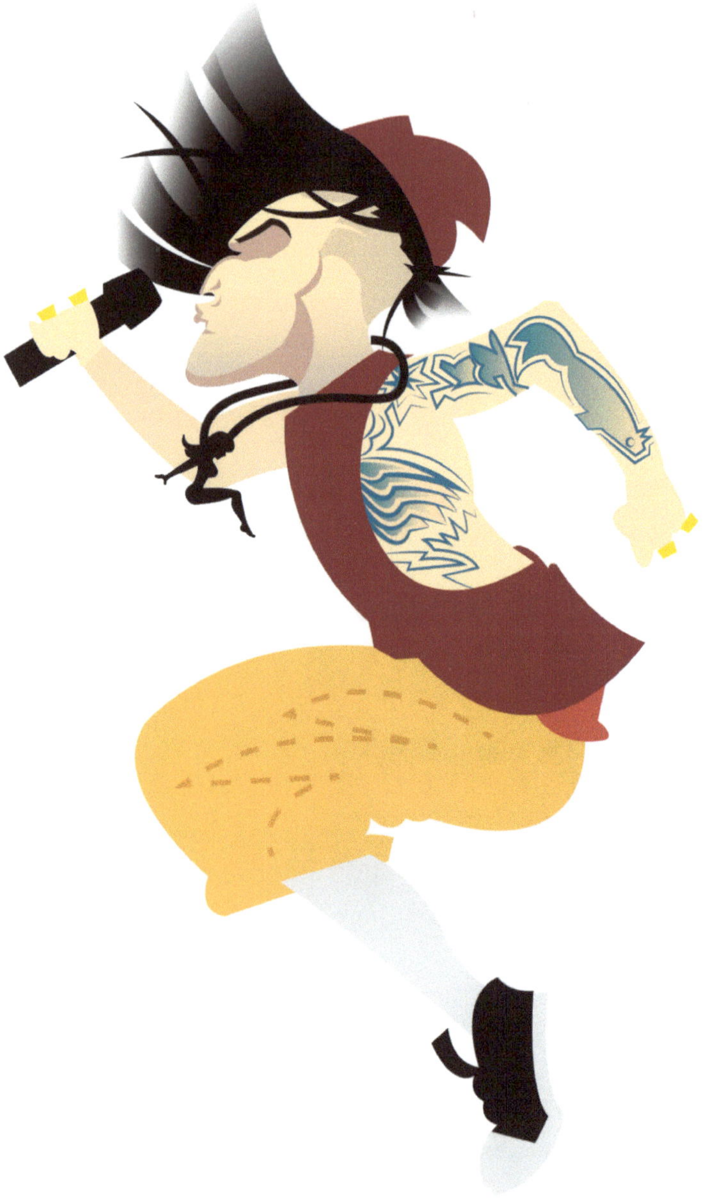

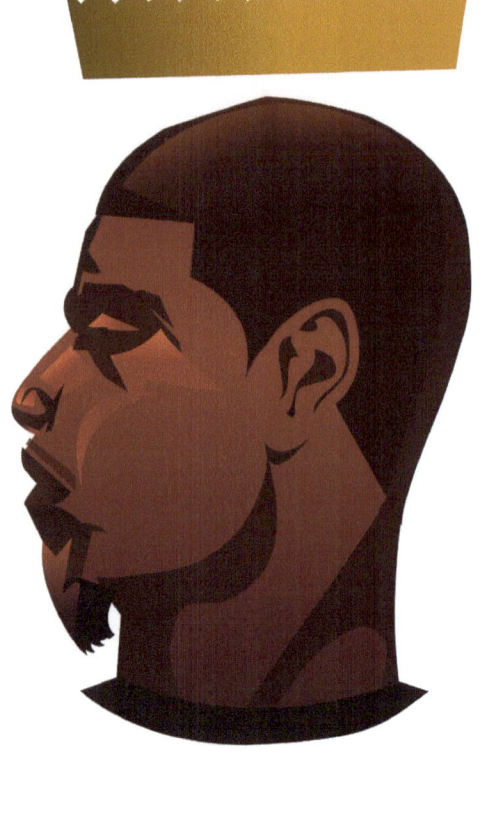

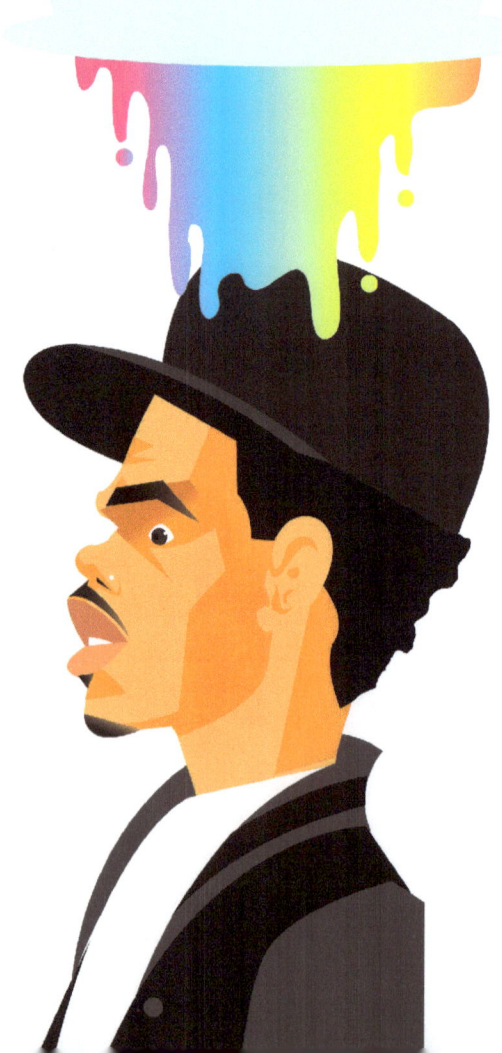

YELAWOLF, BIG KRIT,
CHANCE THE RAPPER

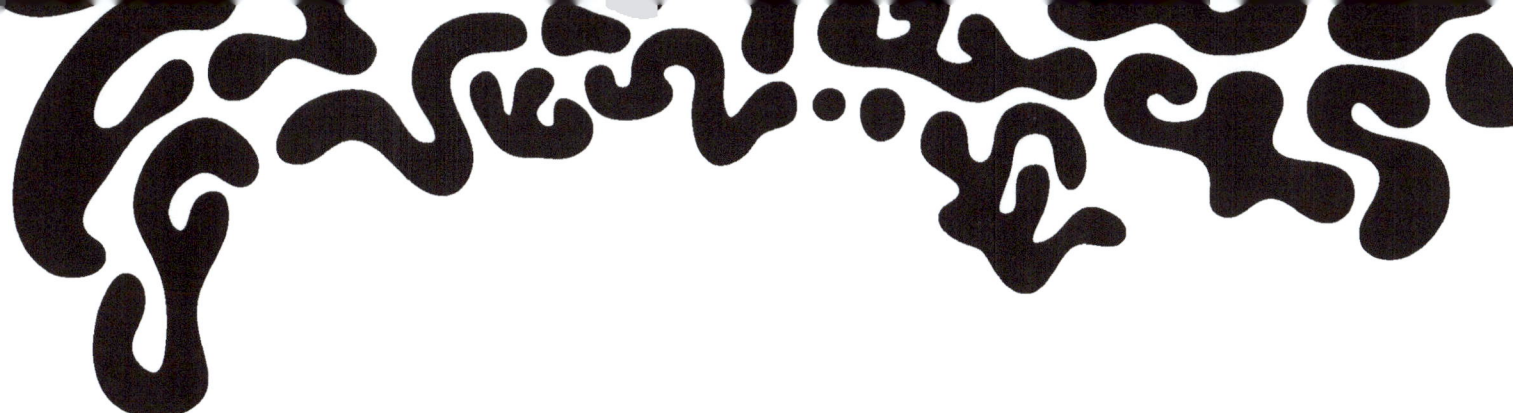

LEADERS OF THE NEW SCHOOL

THE LEADERS OF THE NEW SCHOOL IS AN ON-GOING SERIES THAT FEATURES THE FACES OF RAP AND HIP-HOP AS IT STANDS TODAY. I LOOK AT THIS SERIES AS AN UNFINISHED DOCUMENTARY, SHOWING THE ARTISTS WHO SEEM TO BE THE LEADERS OF THE NEXT MOVEMENT IN HIP-HOP.

Cxpayne   EDIT

"Yes, I'm an artist, but I maintain the fact that I'm a student of Hip-Hop. I graduated from Stankonia High in 2005. I got my Bachelor's degree from A Tribe Called Quest. I'm a UGK alumni. I got my MBA from Russell Simmons. I studied aeronautics with 8 Ball and MJG, concentrating on Starships and Rockets. I took a feminism course under the tutelage of Queen Latifah an MC Lyte. My African American History class was taught by the Goodie Mobb. By the way, the Dungeon Family is my Wu Tang. Yes, I'm an artist, but I maintain the fact that I'm a student of Hip-Hop."

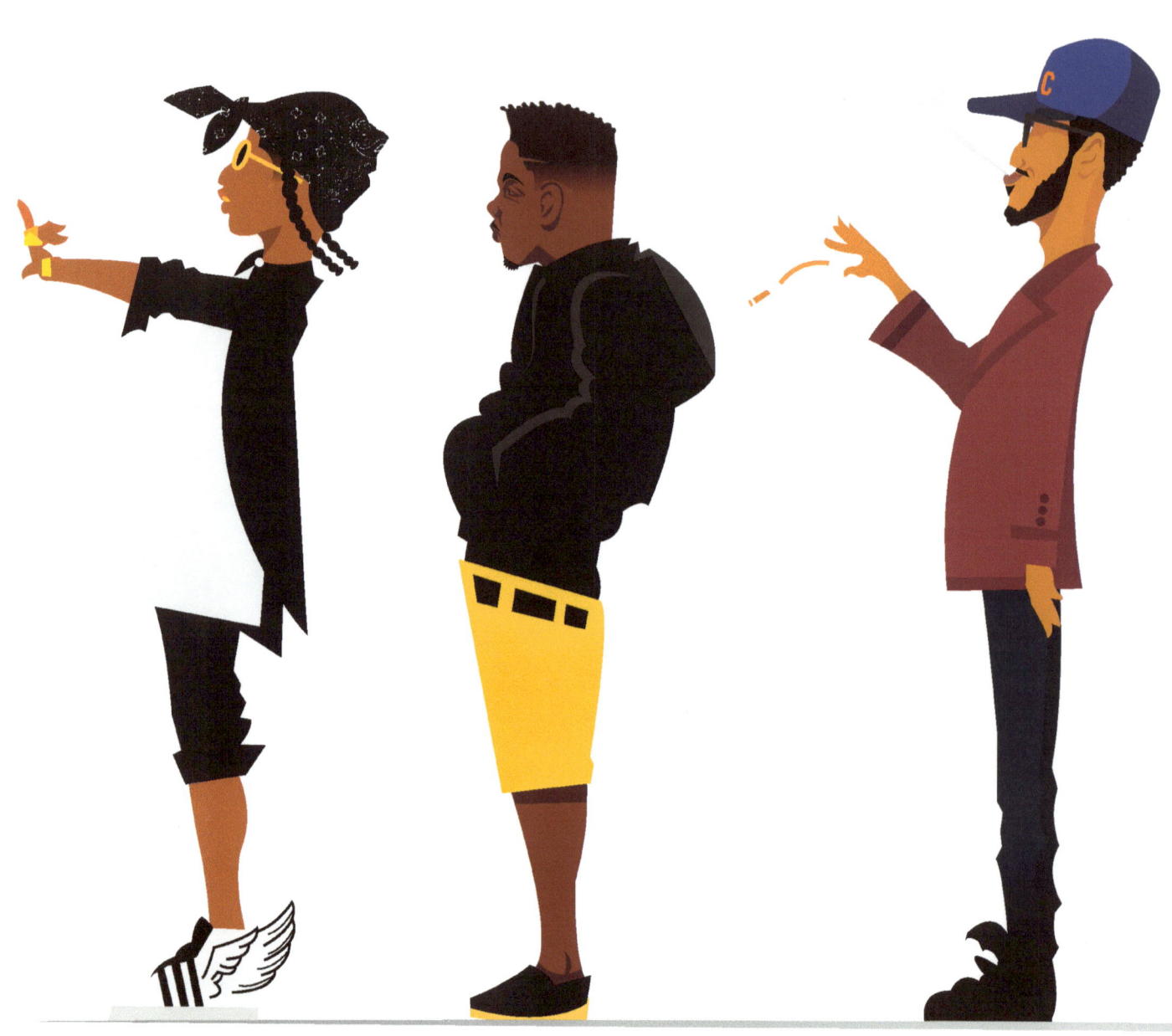

ASAP ROCKY   KENDRICK LAMAR   KID CUDI

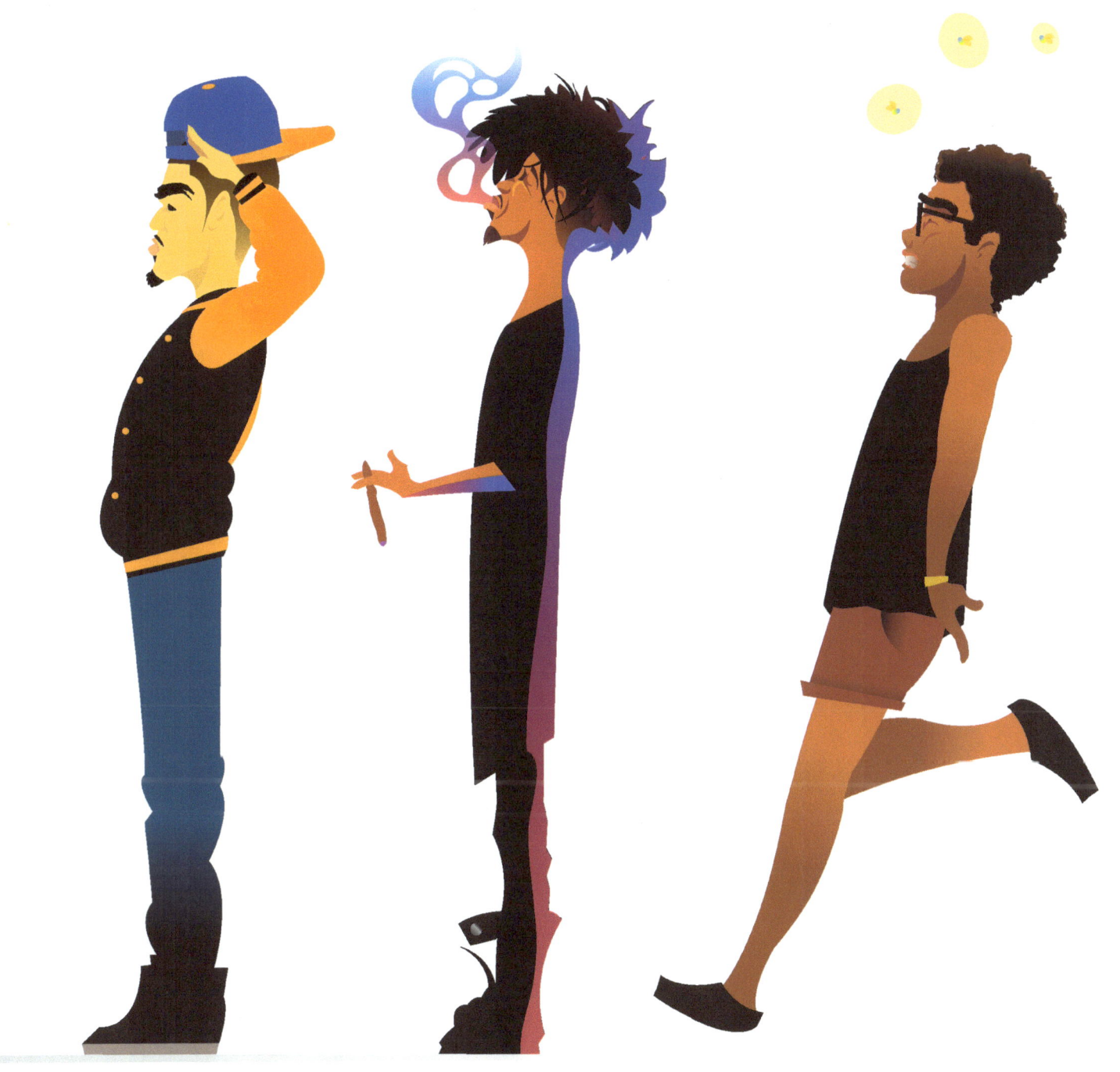

J. COLE   DANNY BROWN   CHILDISH GAMBINO

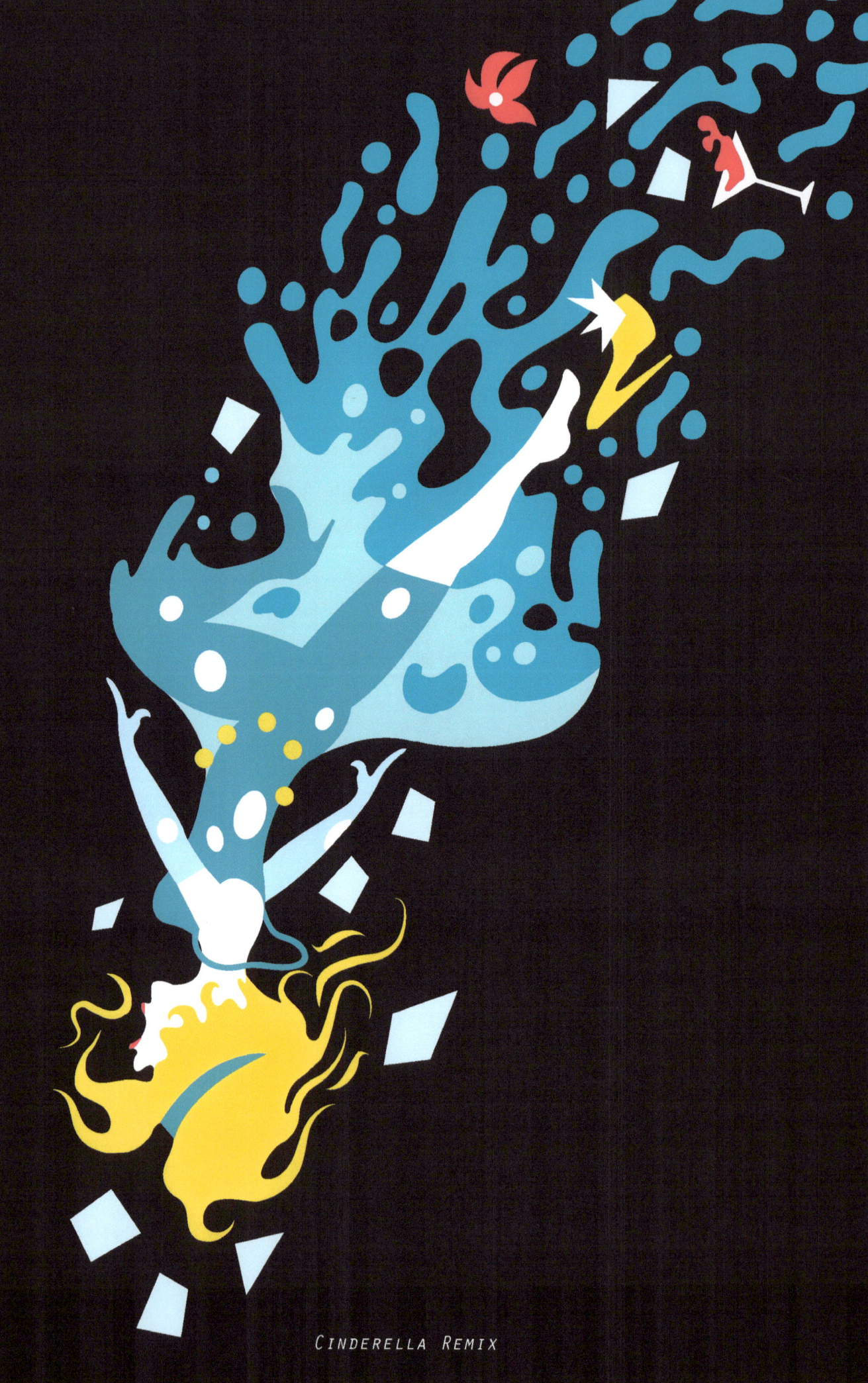

CINDERELLA REMIX

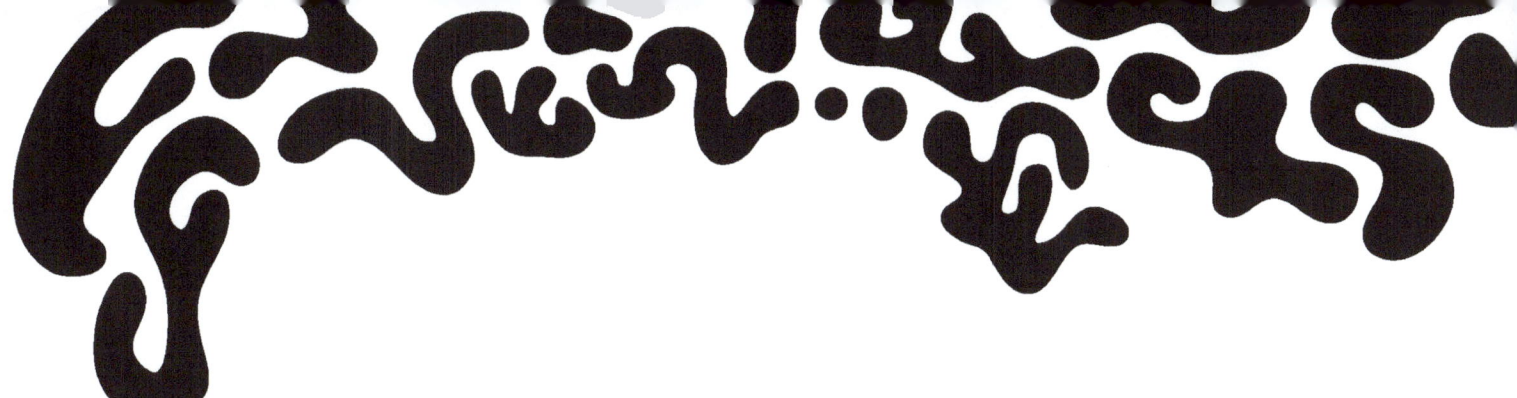

THE ART OF STORIES

WRITERS PAINT PICTURES WITH WORDS. ARTISTS TELL STORIES WITH
PICTURES. I AM A STORY-TELLER AND AN ILLUSTRATOR. THE FOLLOWING IS
A COLLECTION OF ORIGINAL ILLUSTRATIONS OF ORIGINAL IDEAS.

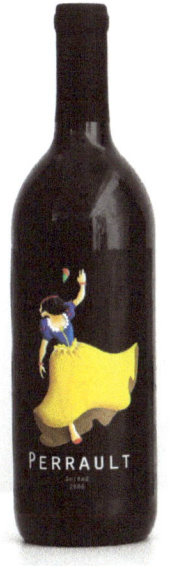 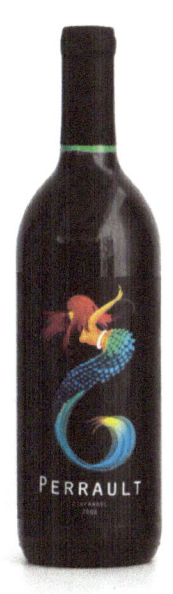 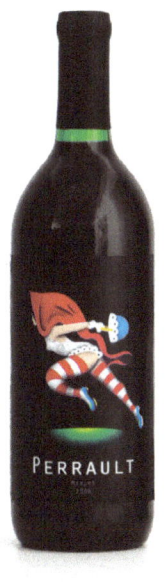 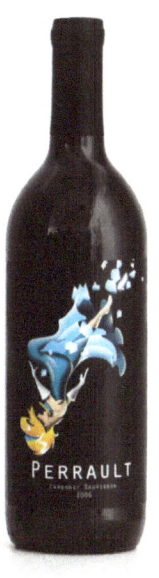

CHARLES PERRAULT WINE BOTTLE SERIES FEATURING SNOW WHITE,
THE LITTLE MERMAID, RED RIDING HOOD, AND CINDERELLA

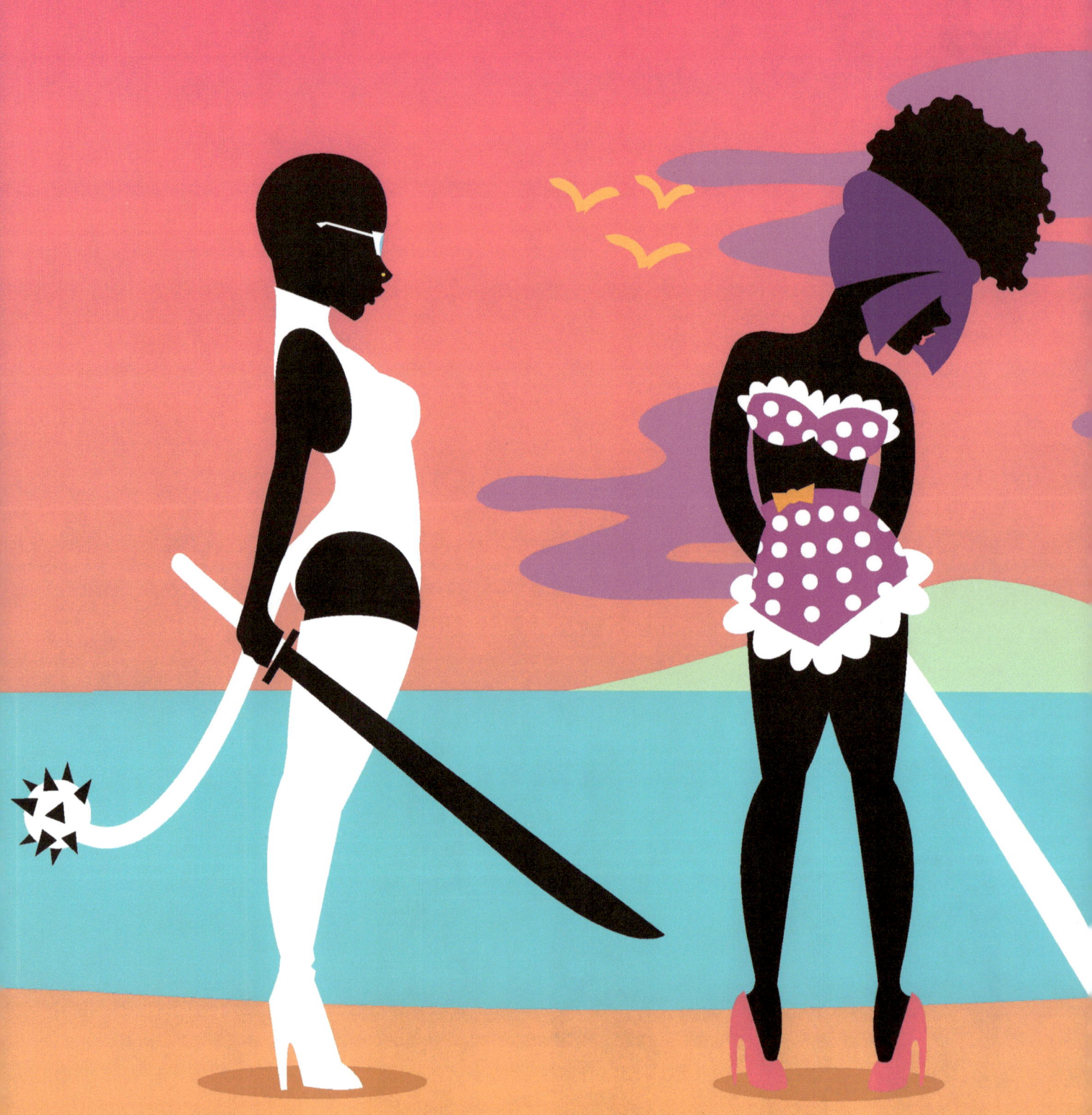

NIKITA KNIVES   SASHA SAMURAI

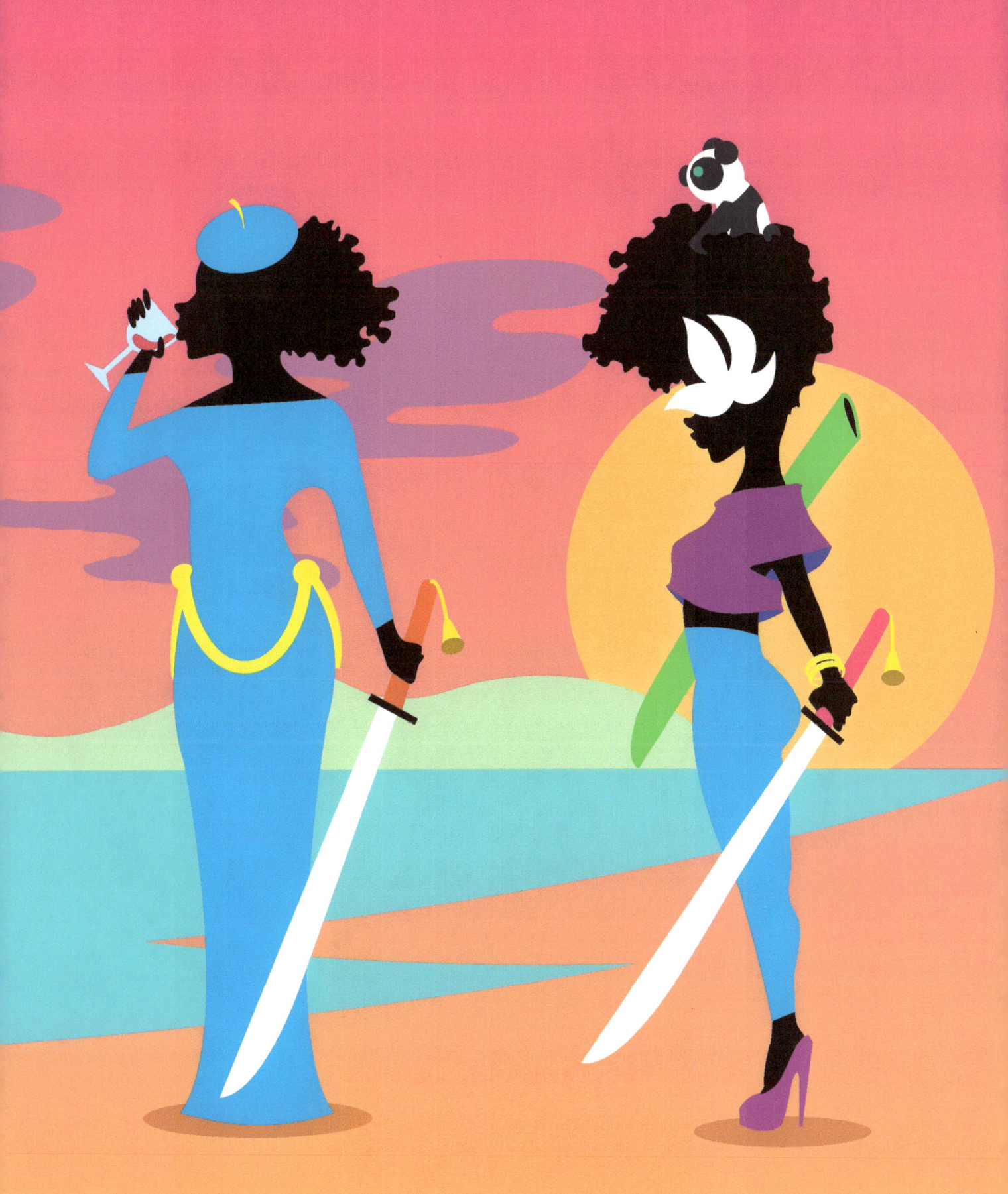

KATRINA KATANA

BUSHIDO BETTY

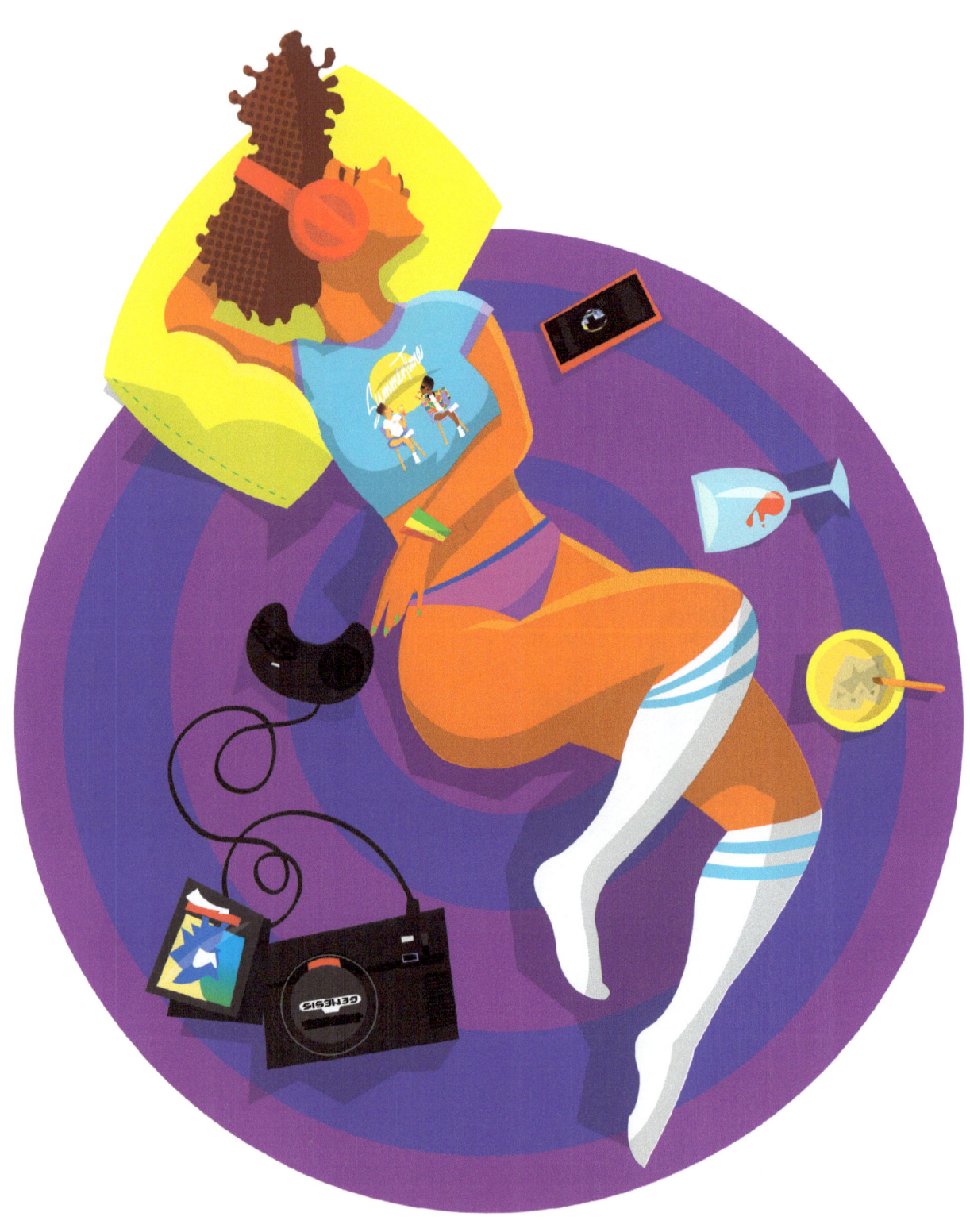

DOWN-TIME

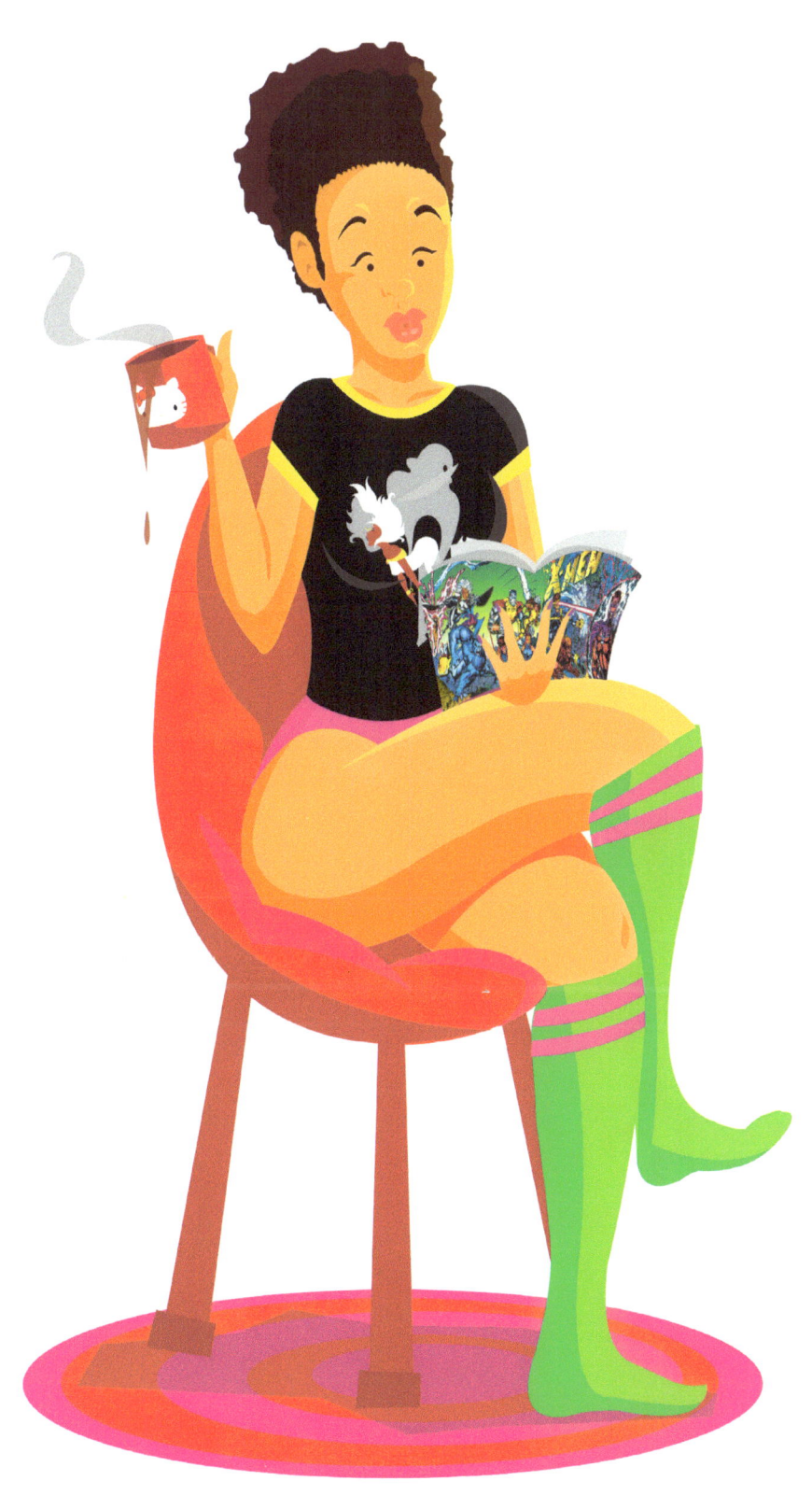

DOWN-TIME #2

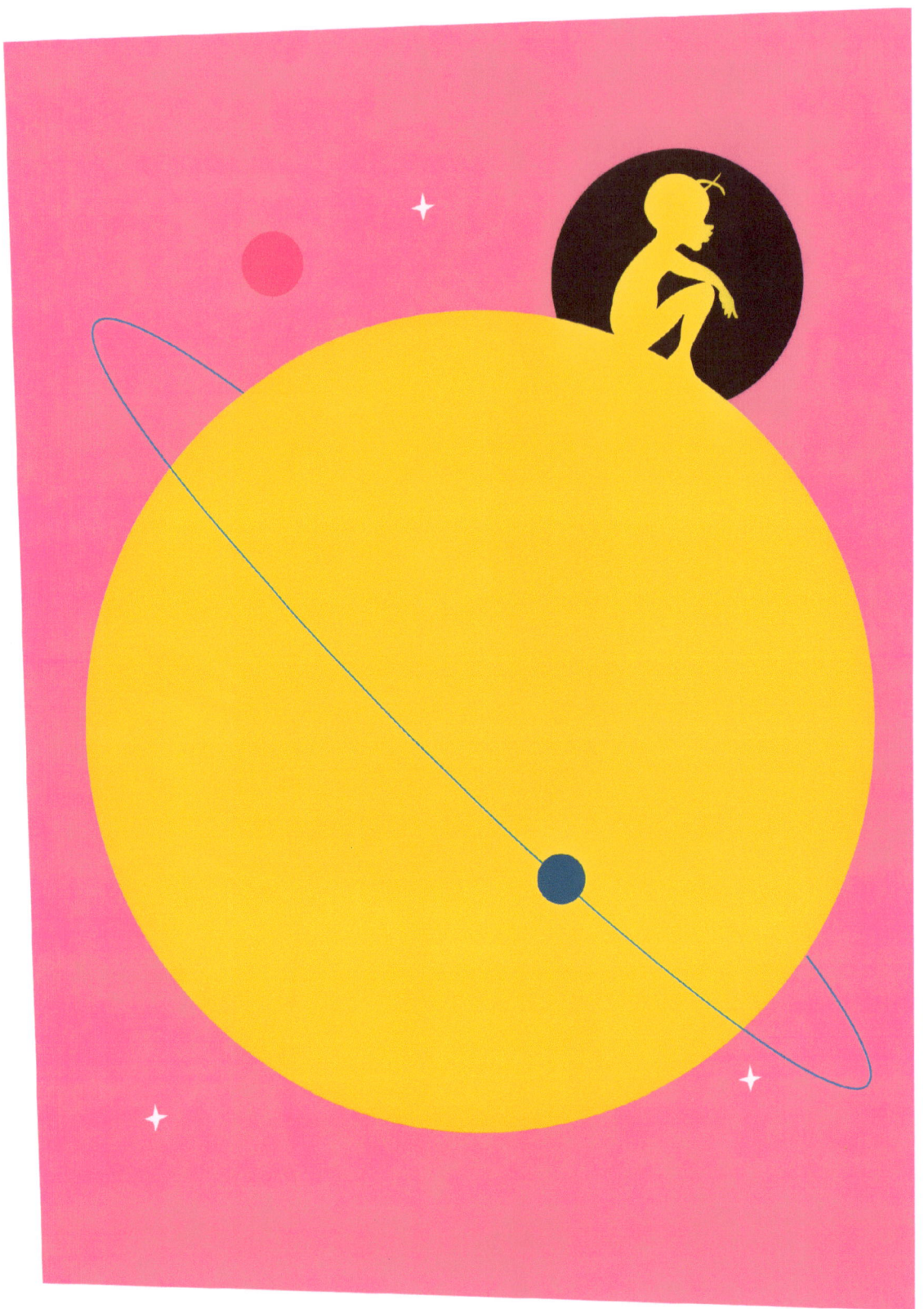

MAN ON THE MOON

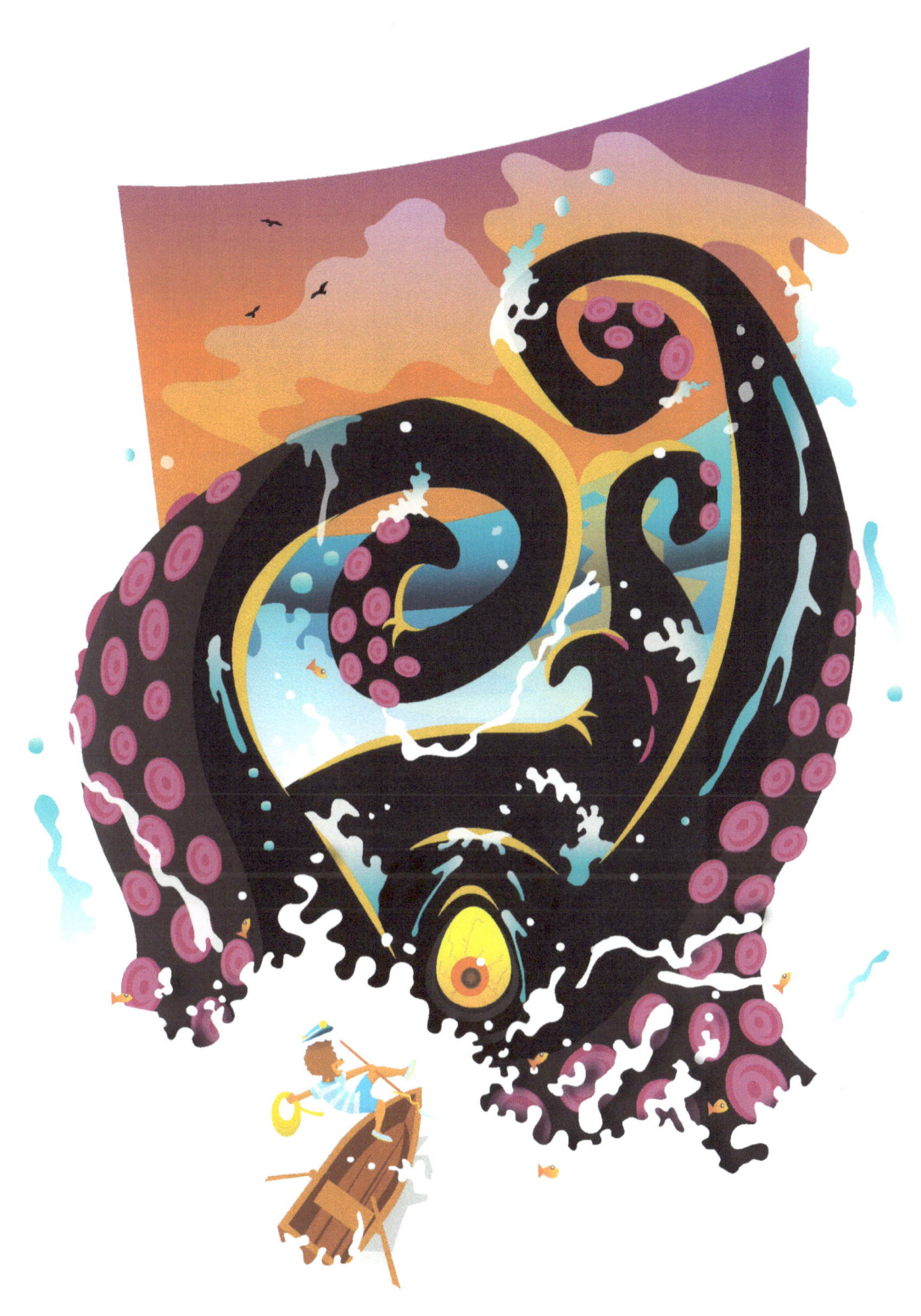

BIG BOUY VS OCTO-DANGER!

Sasha's new move

I remember my Sasha Thumper. She was a dancer. Now that I mention it, they were always dancers.

One evening, she was going on about her dance lessons, and this "new move" she learned. I had to agree to dance with her before she showed me, though. I said yes, knowing my two left feet were like, "NOOOOOO!"

I lasted about ten seconds before landing on my butt. My very awkward butt. Sasha stood over me, laughed and said,

"Ok, ok. I guess you earned an exclusive Ballet performance from Moi!"

"Moi?"

"Me!"

"Oh."

She danced, but I think most of it wasn't even Ballet. It was still great though. Then she did this move, you know, when ballerinas stand on their toes. Her arms and left leg slowly lifted, like she was being pulled my strings. She came to a pause, shook a little bit, and caught herself before she fell.

"TA-DA!" She said and bowed. I applauded.

"SASHA! Time to come in!" Her Mother's voice from her house.

"Bye," She said.

"Bye," I said.

That moment is sitting on my memory's shoreline. I don't remember the name of the street we lived on. I don't remember what I did later on that night. I don't remember the overture that the Traveling Cricket Symphony played or how many stars were out. I remember Sasha's new move.

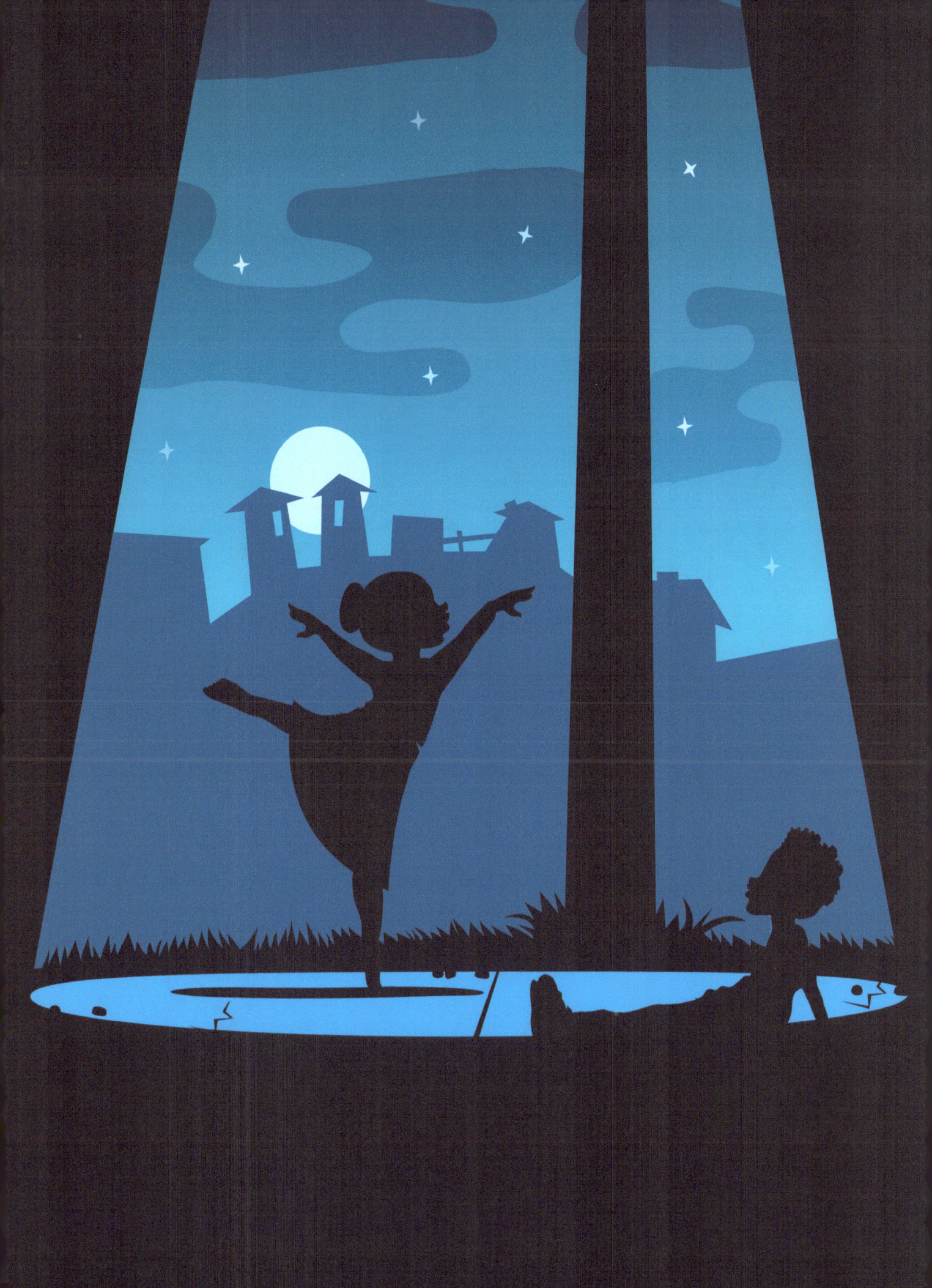

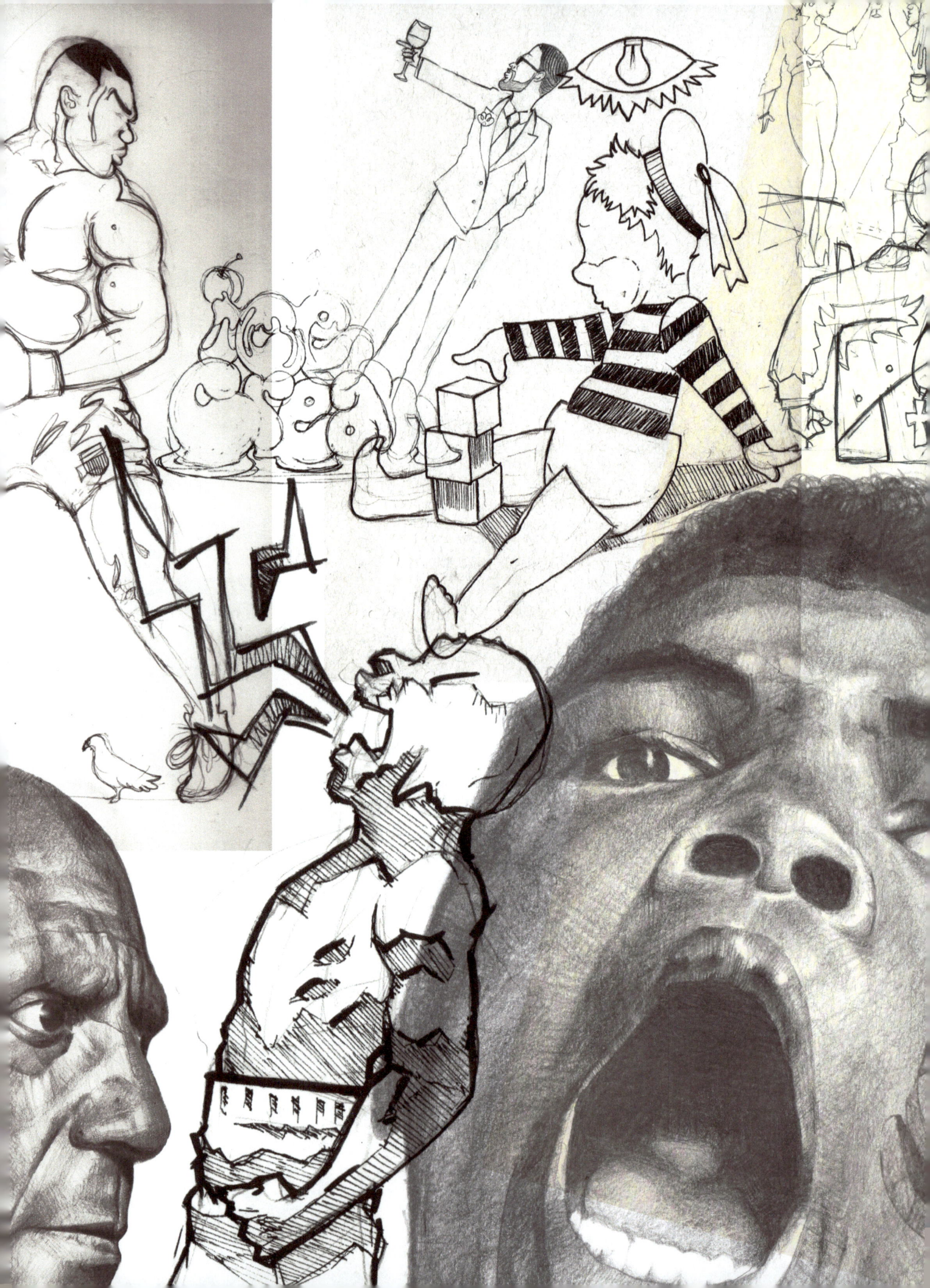

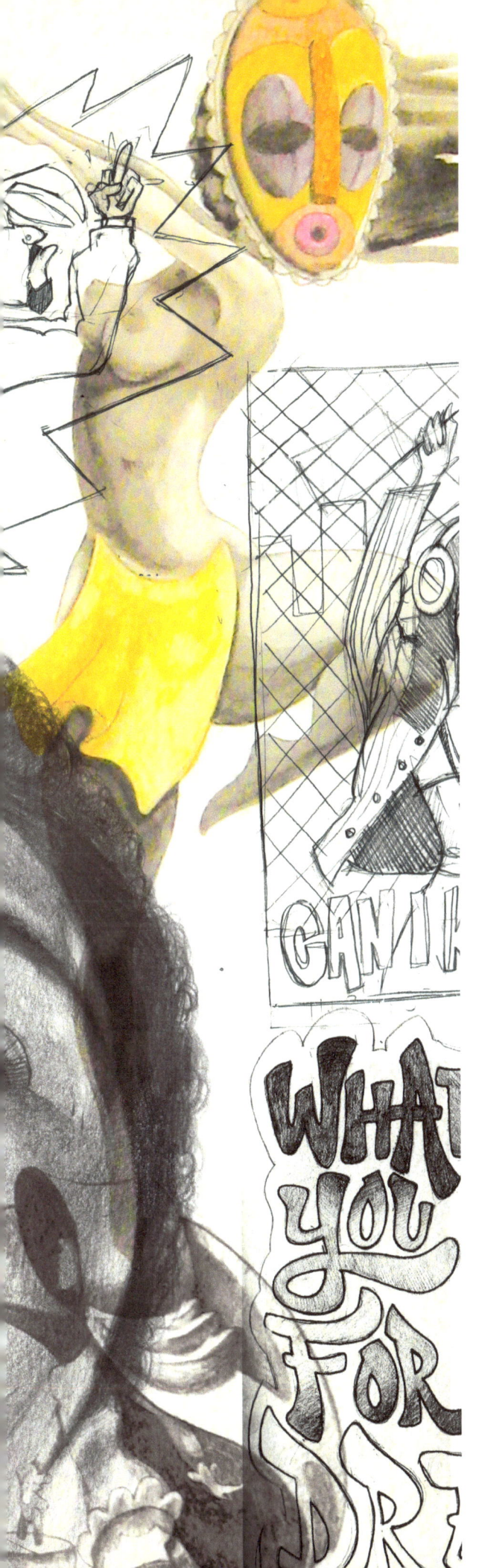

"I DRAW ALL THE TIME. WHEN I'M HAPPY, I DRAW. WHEN I'M SAD, I DRAW. I DRAW WHEN ITS RAINING. I DRAW WHEN ITS HOT. WHEN LIFE GETS TOUGH I DRAW. WHEN I GET TIRED OF DRAWING, I PUT THE PENCIL DOWN, THEN I PICK A PENCIL UP, AND DRAW. I DRAW IN MY SLEEP. I DRAW WHEN I READ. I DRAW."

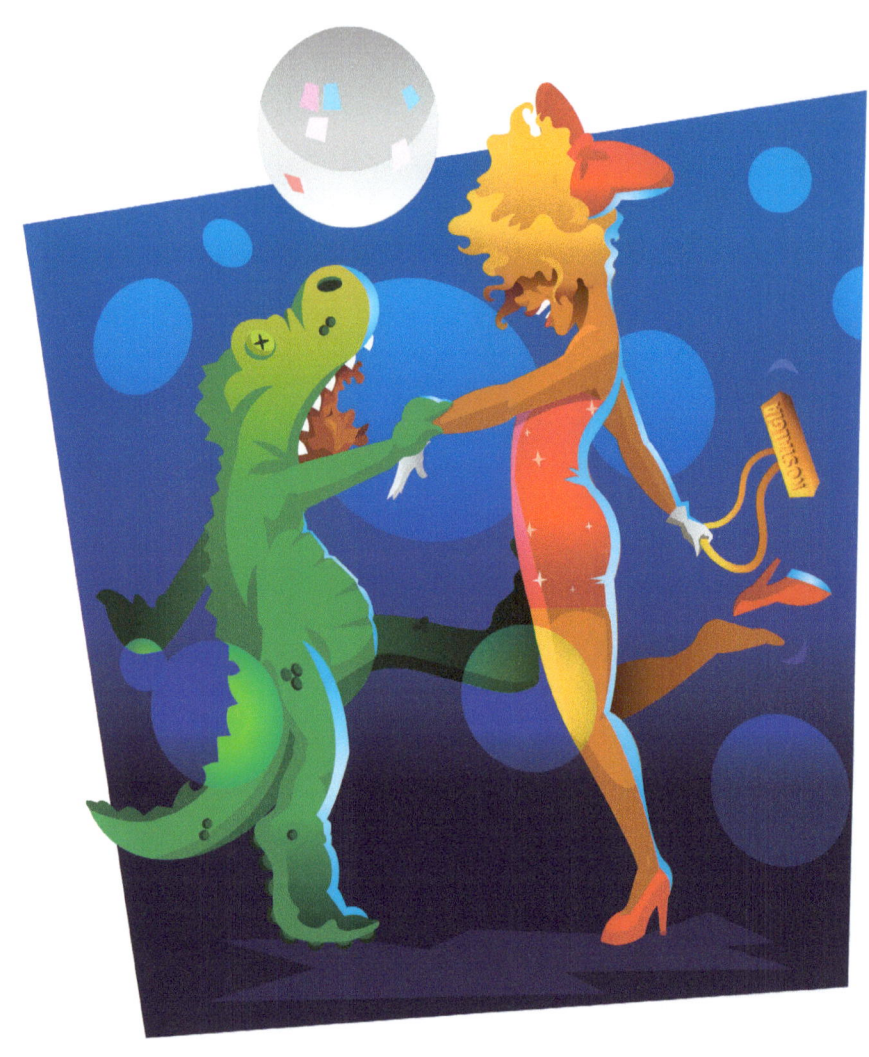

I REMEMBER WHEN RAP WAS YOUNG

ME AND SUSIE HAD SO MUCH FUN

HOLDIN' HANDS AND SKIPPING STONES

HAD AN ALL BLUE CHEVY AND A PLACE OF OUR OWN

BUT THE BIGGEST THRILL WE EVER GOT

WAS DOING A THING CALLED THE CROCODILE ROC

WHILE THE OTHER KIDS WERE ALL PLAYIN POP

WE WERE HOPPIN' AND BOPPIN' TO THE CROCODILE ROC

WELL

CROC-ROCK

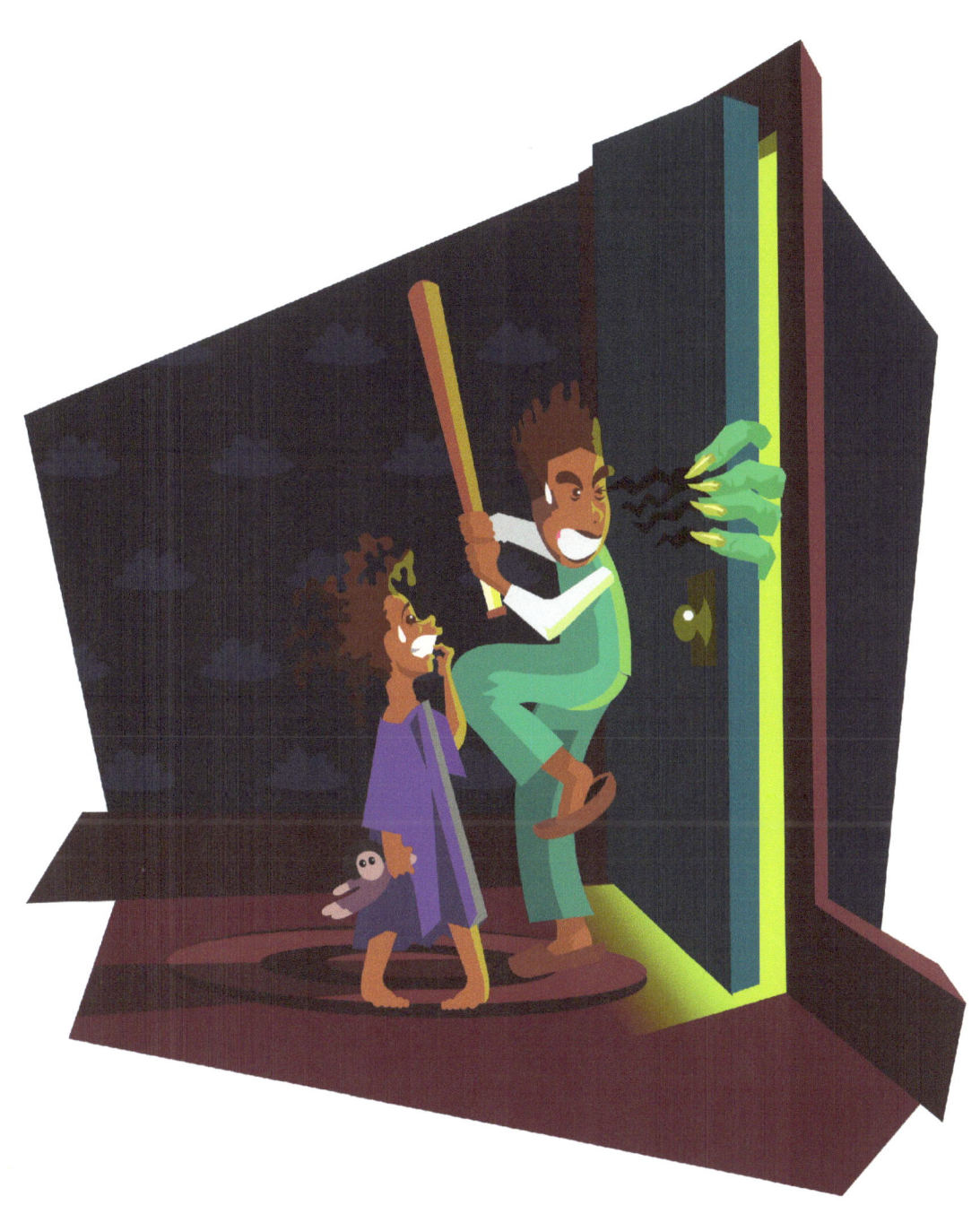

ISAIAH: THE BOOGEYMAN SLAYER

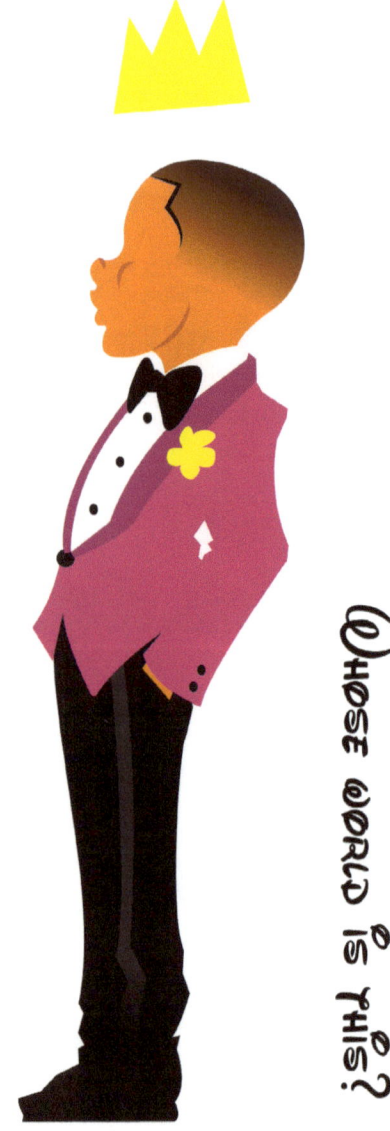

WHOSE WORLD IS THIS?

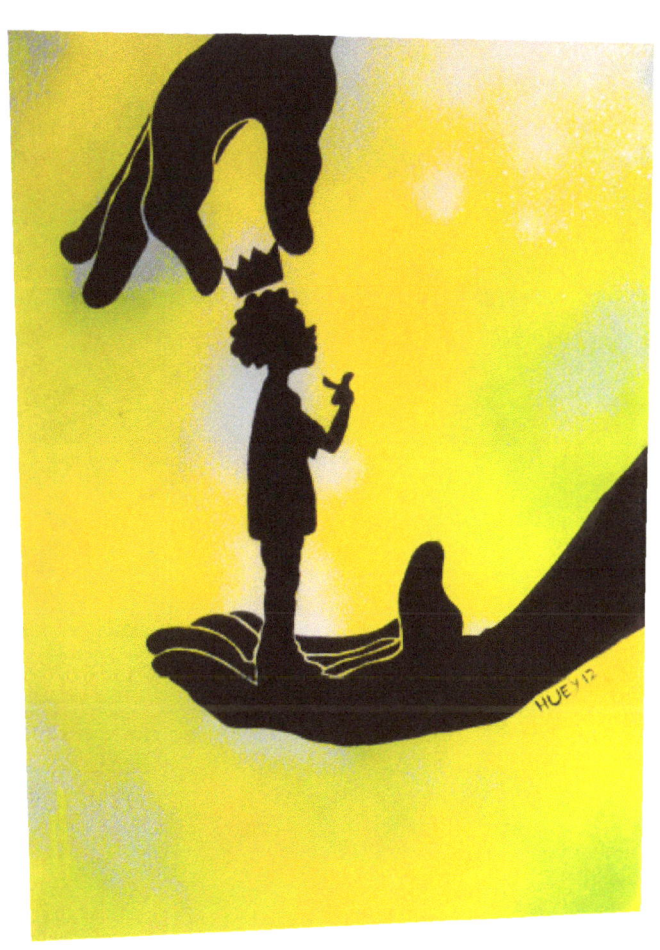

THE CHOSEN

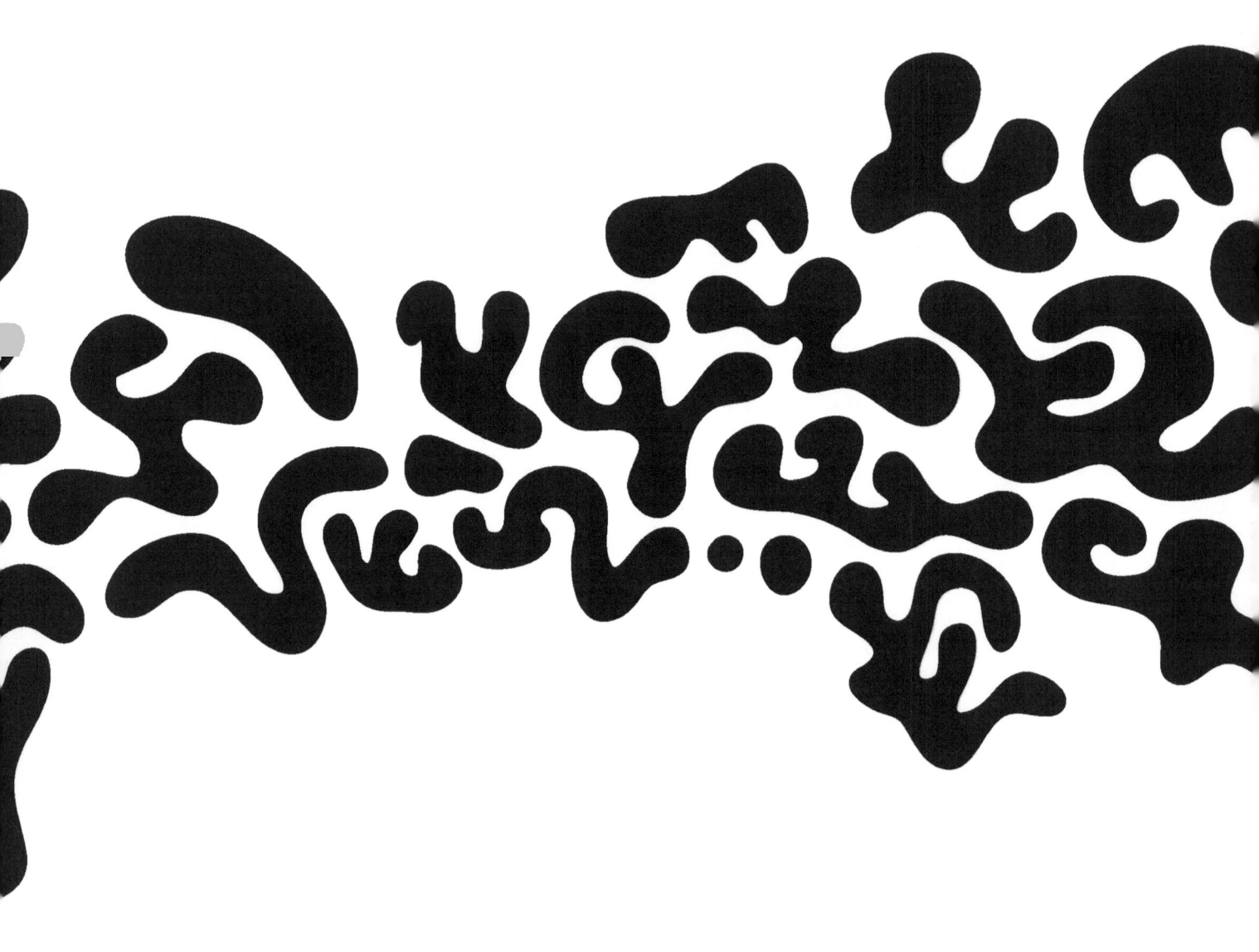

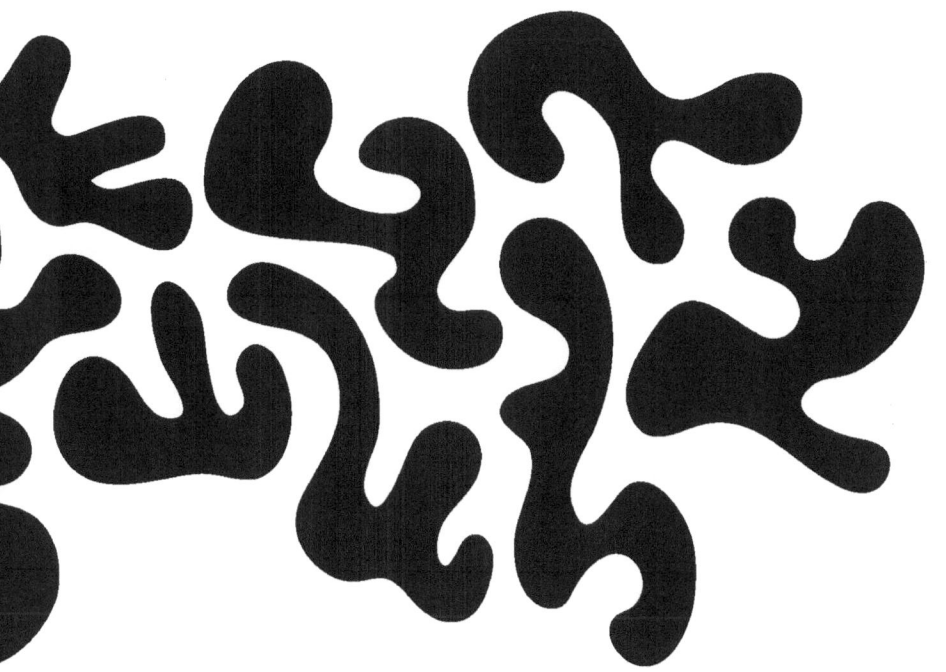

It could be so simple.

Thank you.

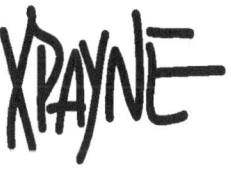

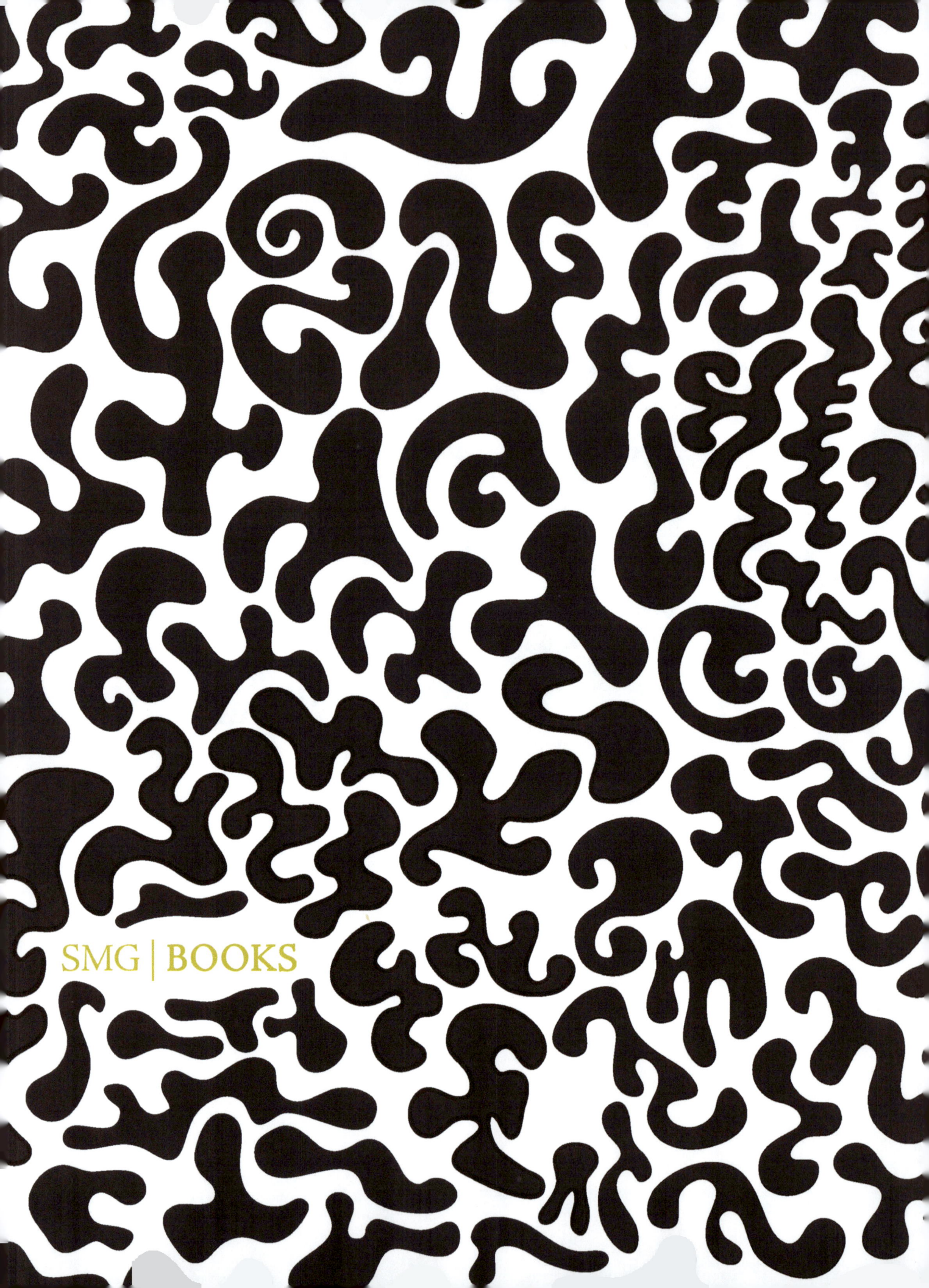

SMG | BOOKS

www.ingramcontent.com/pod-product-compliance
Lightning Source LLC
Chambersburg PA
CBHW050749180526
45159CB00003B/1400